بسم الله الرحمن الرحيم

To The Reader

The reason why a special chapter is assigned to the collapse of the theory of evolution is that this theory constitutes the basis of all anti-spiritual philosophies. Since Darwinism rejects the fact of creation, and therefore the existence of God, during the last 140 years it has caused many people to abandon their faith or fall into doubt. Therefore, showing that this theory is a deception is a very important duty, which is strongly related to the religion (*deen*). It is imperative that this important service be rendered to everyone. Some of our readers may find the chance to read only one of our books. Therefore, we think it appropriate to spare a chapter for a summary of this subject.

In all the books by the author, faith-related issues are explained in the light of the Qur'anic verses and people are invited to learn God's words and to live by them. All the subjects that concern God's verses are explained in such a way as to leave no room for doubt or question marks in the reader's mind. The sincere, plain and fluent style employed ensures that everyone of every age and from every social group can easily understand the books. This effective and lucid narrative makes it possible to read them in a single sitting. Even those who rigorously reject spirituality are influenced by the facts recounted in these books and cannot refute the truthfulness of their contents.

This book and all the other works of the author can be read individually or discussed in a group at a time of conversation. Those readers who are willing to profit from the books will find discussion very useful in the sense that they will be able to relate their own reflections and experiences to one another.

In addition, it will be a great service to the religion to contribute to the presentation and reading of these books, which are written solely for the good pleasure of God. All the books of the author are extremely convincing. For this reason, for those who want to communicate the religion to other people, one of the most effective methods is to encourage them to read these books.

It is hoped that the reader will take time to look through the review of other books on the final pages of the book, and appreciate the rich source of material on faith-related issues, which are very useful
and a pleasure to read.

In these books, you will not find, as in some other books, the personal views of the author, explanations based on dubious sources, styles that are unobservant of the respect and reverence due to sacred subjects, nor hopeless, doubt-creating, and pessimistic accounts that create deviations in the heart.

ISLAM DENOUNCES TERRORISM

God calls to the Abode of Peace and He guides whom He wills to a straight path.
(Qur'an, 10:25)

HARUN YAHYA

January, 2002

Amal Press
PO BOX 688 Bristol BS99 3ZR
England

About The Author

The author, who writes under the pen-name HARUN YAHYA, was born in Ankara in 1956. Having completed his primary and secondary education in Ankara, he then studied arts at Istanbul's Mimar Sinan University and philosophy at Istanbul University. Since the 1980s, the author has published many books on political, faith-related and scientific issues. Harun Yahya is well-known as an author who has written very important works disclosing the imposture of evolutionists, the invalidity of their claims and the dark liaisons between Darwinism and bloody ideologies.

His pen-name is made up of the names "Harun" (Aaron) and "Yahya" (John), in memory of the two esteemed prophets who fought against lack of faith. The Prophet's seal on the cover of the author's books has a symbolic meaning linked to the their contents. This seal represents the Qur'an as the last Book by God and the last word of Him and our Prophet, the last of all the prophets. Under the guidance of the Qur'an and Sunnah, the author makes it his main goal to disprove each one of the fundamental tenets of godless ideologies and to have the "last word", so as to completely silence the objections raised against religion. The seal of the Prophet, who attained ultimate wisdom and moral perfection, is used as a sign of his intention of saying this last word.

All these works by the author centre around one goal: to convey the message of the Qur'an to people, thus encouraging them to think about basic faith-related issues, such as the existence of God, His unity and the hereafter, and to display the decrepit foundations and perverted works of godless systems.

Harun Yahya enjoys a wide readership in many countries, from India to America, England to Indonesia, Poland to Bosnia, and Spain to Brazil. Some of his books are available in English, French, German, Italian, Portuguese, Urdu, Arabic, Albanian, Russian, Serbo-Croat (Bosnian), Uygur Turkish, and Indonesian, and they have been enjoyed by readers all over the world.

Greatly appreciated all around the world, these works have been instrumental in many people putting their faith in God and in many others gaining a deeper insight into their faith. The wisdom, and the sincere and easy-to-understand style employed give these books a distinct touch which directly strikes any one who reads or examines them. Immune to objections, these works are characterised by their features of rapid effectiveness, definite results and irrefutability. It is unlikely that those who read these books and give a serious thought to them can any longer sincerely advocate the materialistic philosophy, atheism and any other perverted ideology or philosophy. Even if they continue to advocate, this will be only a sentimental insistence since these books have refuted these ideologies from their very basis. All contemporary movements of denial are ideologically defeated today, thanks to the collection of books written by Harun Yahya.

There is no doubt that these features result from the wisdom and lucidity of the Qur'an. The author certainly does not feel proud of himself; he merely intends to serve as a means in one's search for God's right path. Furthermore, no material gain is sought in the publication of these works.

Considering these facts, those who encourage people to read these books, which open the "eyes" of the heart and guide them in becoming more devoted servants of God, render an invaluable service.

Meanwhile, it would just be a waste of time and energy to propagate books which create confusion in peoples' minds, lead man into ideological chaos, and which, clearly have no strong and precise effects in removing the doubts in peoples' hearts, as also verified from previous experience. It is apparent that it is impossible for books devised to emphasize the author's literary power rather than the noble goal of saving people from loss of faith, to have such a great effect. Those who doubt this can readily see that the sole aim of Harun Yahya's books is to overcome disbelief and to disseminate the moral values of the Qur'an. The success, impact and sincerity this service has attained are manifest in the reader's conviction.

One point needs to be kept in mind: The main reason for the continuing cruelty and conflict, and all the ordeals Muslims undergo is the ideological prevalence of disbelief. These things can only come to an end with the ideological defeat of disbelief and by ensuring that everybody knows about the wonders of creation and Qur'anic morality, so that people can live by it. Considering the state of the world today, which forces people into the downward spiral of violence, corruption and conflict, it is clear that this service has to be provided more speedily and effectively. Otherwise, it may be too late.

It is no exaggeration to say that the collection of books by Harun Yahya have assumed this leading role. By the Will of God, these books will be the means through which people in the 21st century will attain the peace and bliss, justice and happiness promised in the Qur'an.

The works of the author include The New Masonic Order, The Disasters Darwinism Brought to Humanity, Communism in Ambush, The Bloody Ideology of Darwinism: Fascism, The 'Secret Hand' in Bosnia, Behind the Scenes of Terrorism, Solution: The Morals of the Qur'an, Articles 1-2-3, A Weapon of Satan: Romantism, Truths 1-2, The Western World Turns to God, The Evolution Deceit, Precise Answers to Evolutionists, Evolutionary Falsehoods, Perished Nations, For Men of Understanding, The Prophet Moses, The Prophet Joseph, The Golden Age, Allah's Artistry in Colour, Glory is Everywhere, The Truth of the Life of This World, Knowing the Truth, Eternity Has Already Begun, Timelessness and the Reality of Fate, The Dark Magic of Darwinism, The Religion of Darwinism, The Collapse of the Theory of Evolution in 20 Questions, Allah is Known Through Reason, The Qur'an Leads the Way to Science, The Real Origin of Life, Consciousness in the Cell, A String of Miracles, The Creation of the Universe, Miracles of the Qur'an, The Design in Nature, Self-Sacrifice and Intelligent Behaviour Models in Animals, The End of Darwinism, Deep Thinking, Never Plead Ignorance, The Green Miracle Photosynthesis, The Miracle in the Cell, The Miracle in the Eye, The Miracle in the Spider, The Miracle in the Gnat, The Miracle in the Ant, The Miracle of the Immune System, The Miracle of Creation in Plants, The Miracle in the Atom, The Miracle in the Honeybee, The Miracle of Seed, The Miracle of Hormone, The Miracle of the Termite, The Miracle of the Human Being, The Miracle of Man's Creation, The Miracle of Protein, The Secrets of DNA.

The author's childrens books are: Children Darwin Was Lying!, The World of Animals, The Splendour in the Skies, Wonderful Creatures, Let us Learn Our Religion, The World of Our Little Friends: The Ants, Honeybees That Build Perfect Combs, Skillful Dam Builders: Beavers.

The author's other works on Quranic topics include: The Basic Concepts in the Qur'an, The Moral Values of the Qur'an, Quick Grasp of Faith 1-2-3, Ever Thought About the Truth?, Crude Understanding of Disbelief, Devoted to Allah, Abandoning the Society of Ignorance, The Real Home of Believers: Paradise, Knowledge of the Qur'an, Qur'an Index, Emigrating for the Cause of Allah, The Character of the Hypocrite in the Qur'an, The Secrets of the Hypocrite, The Names of Allah, Communicating the Message and Disputing in the Qur'an, Answers from the Qur'an, Death Resurrection Hell, The Struggle of the Messengers, The Avowed Enemy of Man: Satan, The Greatest Slander: Idolatry, The Religion of the Ignorant, The Arrogance of Satan, Prayer in the Qur'an, The Importance of Conscience in the Qur'an, The Day of Resurrection, Never Forget, Disregarded Judgements of the Qur'an, Human Characters in the Society of Ignorance, The Importance of Patience in the Qur'an, General Information from the Qur'an, The Mature Faith, Before You Regret, Our Messengers Say, The Mercy of Believers, The Fear of Allah, The Nightmare of Disbelief, Jesus Will Return, Beauties Presented by the Qur'an for Life, A Bouquet of the Beauties of Allah 1-2-3-4, The Iniquity Called "Mockery", The Mystery of the Test, The True Wisdom According to the Qur'an, The Struggle with the Religion of Irreligion, The School of Yusuf, The Alliance of the Good, Slanders Spread Against Muslims Throughout History, The Importance of Following the Good Word, Why Do You Deceive Yourself?, Islam: The Religion of Ease, Enthusiasm and Excitement in the Qur'an, Seeing Good in Everything, How do the Unwise Interpret the Qur'an?, Some Secrets of the Qur'an, The Courage of Believers, Being Hopeful in the Qur'an, Justice and Tolerance in the Qur'an, Basic Tenets of Islam, Those Who do not Listen to the Qur'an.

First English Edition published in January 2002

Published by
Amal Press
PO BOX 688
Bristol
BS99 3ZR
England
Website: http://www.amalpress.com
E-mail: info@amalpress.com

By Harun Yahya
Translated by: Carl Rossini and Ron Evans
Edited by Aftab A. Malik

A Catalog Record of this book is available from the British Library
ISBN: 0-9540544-1-5

Special thanks to F.A Khan, Zain ul-Abedin and Hammayun, 'Ali.

All translations from the Qur'an are from "The Noble Qur'an: a New
Rendering of its Meaning in English"
by Hajj Abdalhaqq and Aisha Bewley, published by Bookwork,
Norwich, UK. 1420 CE/1999 AH.

Website:
www.harunyahya.com
www.hyahya.org
www.islamdenouncesterrorism.com

FOREWORD

"We have made you a Middle Nation"
(Holy Qur'an, Surat al-Baqara:143)

SEPTEMBER 11

Since the horrific and tragic events of September 11th, nothing has been more discussed and scrutinised in the public arena than Islam. The world at large has been subjected to a wealth of analysis by 'experts' which has further fuelled people's curiosity about this religion. Book-sellers in Europe and the Middle East have reported an upsurge in interest in the Qur'an, which confirms what one British newspaper editor had to say: 'Islam [..] has never been of greater interest to the people of Britain than it is today.'[1] In America, where there are some six million Muslims, Islam is said to be the nation's fastest growing religion, despite there being no systematic form of missionary work.[2]

Contrary to official praise of Islam by the President of America and the Prime Minister of England, some of the media have bluntly suggested that the action taken after September's event is a war and Islam is at its heart. Despite there being a conscious effort to truly understand Islam and Muslims, there seem to be those who are determined to paint terrorism and Islam with the same brush. Simplified and undifferentiated descriptions of Islam help create an image by which Islam is seen as hostile to Western culture, and a religion of backwardness and oppression. 'A selective presentation and analysis of Islam and events by both scholars and political commentators too often inform articles and editorials on the Muslim world', says John Esposito, Director of the Center for Muslim-Christian Understanding, at Georgetown University in Washington. 'This selective analysis fails to tell the whole story […] While it sheds some light, it is a partial light that obscures and distorts the full picture.'[3]

The world community shares this small planet with the Muslim community which comprises some 1.2 billion adherents to the faith, so anyone who understands Islam to be a religion of terror would naturally be concerned. However, these fears are not well-grounded. Writing in Time magazine, Karen Armstrong asserts that: 'If the evil carnage we witnessed on September 11 were typical of the faith, and Islam truly inspired and justified such violence, its growth and the increasing presence of Muslims in both Europe and the U.S. would be a terrifying prospect. Fortunately, this is not the case.'[4]

There seems to be a noticeable discrepancy between knowledge of Islam on the one hand and the certainty of judgements on the other. While the terrorist crime of September 11th may have been the work of some misled individuals, it was certainly not the product of Islam. Islam is a religion that preaches peace, compassion, justice, and frowns upon suicide. The kamikaze assault on innocent civilians stood in direct conflict with Islam's most elementary principles, teachings and spirit – one does not need to be an expert to realise this.

ISLAM and TRADITION

If Islam is a religion of peace, why the misunderstanding? How can a religion of peace gain a reputation for being a religion of war and terror? The answer lies in the way that Islamic scriptures are misinterpreted to suit perverted agendas. Words and phrases that are often repeated in the media have been misconstrued by individuals to give incorrect meanings. The deliberate blur between 'jihad' and acts of terror has been a phenomenon that has resulted from those unqualified in the science of Sacred Law.

Since the end of the Sunni Ottoman Caliphate in 1924, the Muslim world has been fragmented. The loss of unification created many difficulties from which Muslims are still trying to recover. For one thing, it has seen the loss of the promulgation of traditional Islam, which has now given way to individuals claiming the right to reinterpret Islamic texts to grant them legitimacy in their own ideas. This has seen a tendency 'toward ambiguity and the careless use of many important terms.'[5] Traditional Islam in contrast is related to the notion of orthodoxy, clarity and authority; to continuity and consistency in the transmission of the truth. It places its reliance upon classical scholarship as exemplified in the four schools of Islamic jurisprudence. Within this tradition of Islam, a true Islamic landscape emerges, encompassing the richness of scholarly tradition and its illuminating contribution to the advancement of civilisation.[6]

Sunni Islam engenders a faith and practice that makes the taking of innocent lives unimaginable and which is shared by the vast majority of Muslims worldwide, however the radicals appear to have overlooked this pivotal pillar with their new interpretations of Sacred Law. As noted by Tim Winter, a lecturer on Islam at the faculty of Divinity at Cambridge University 'One of the unseen, unsung triumphs of true Islam in the modern world is its complete freedom from any terroristic involvement […] Everyone, enemies included, knows that the very idea is absurd.'[7]

The dismantling of the traditional places of learning by the colonialists allowed individuals to make literal and extreme interpretations of Sacred Law that are in contradiction to and radically different from the previous centuries of traditional Islamic practice and learning. Muhammad, the Messenger of God, may God bless him and grant him peace, forewarned of such a time when '[..] people [will] take the ignorant as leaders who are asked for and who give Islamic legal opinion without knowledge [they are] misguided and misguiding.'[8] The result has been examples of extreme religious practice devoid of any real knowledge and characterised by bigotry, intolerance, harshness and excessiveness – all of which are in opposition to Islam as exemplified by the Messenger of God, may God bless him and grant him peace, who always advocated the middle way.

TERRORISM

Muhammad, may God bless him and grant him peace, warned his companions to avoid extremes – which he explained was the cause of the destruction of earlier communities. Terrorists it appears, feel that this injunction does not apply to them. Terrorism is an act against God. Anyone who tries to justify such atrocities ultimately fails, since both the Sacred Law and theology abhor such acts as moral sins that run contrary to the essence of Islam. The Qur'an instructs Muslims in times of adversity to act with justice, perseverance and patience. Terrorists apparently never think of relating their acts to the elementary principle that Islam places great value on: the sanctity of human life. 'If someone kills another person – unless it is in retaliation for someone else or for causing corruption in the earth – it is as if he had murdered all mankind' is a verse of the Qur'an, which is disregarded by the fanaticism of hate.

Traditional Muslim jurists considered terrorist attacks against unsuspecting and defenseless victims as heinous and immoral crimes and treated the perpetrators as the worst type of criminals. It is a well-established Qur'anic precept that the injustice of others does not excuse one's own injustice.[9]

JIHAD

In the West, the term 'jihad' has come to be known as something wholly negative – it has been somewhat simplistically described as waging a holy war against infidels. However, in Islam, jihad is something that is positive. It consists of two dimensions: the inner jihad that seeks to curb negative and self-destructive forces within; and the external jihad which is a struggle against violence and tyranny by means of words and actions. As for the latter, it has strict rules of engagement which prohibit destroying civilian life, harming animals and even chopping down trees.[10]

The former type of jihad, said to be the most important, is that of the inner self. Muhammad, may God bless him and grant him peace, was reported to have said: "The best jihad one performs is that of helping oneself gain more knowledge of Almighty God."[11] On another occasion, the Messenger of God addressed his companions, saying: "We are now returning from the minor jihad to the major jihad (that of the struggle of the inner self.)"

COMPASSION and MERCY

In the context of the current atmosphere of violence, one might be excused for assuming that jihad is one of Islam's main pillars. However, this is far from the truth. Islam is 'not addicted to war,' nor does jihad form any one of the five pillars of faith. On the contrary, the Qur'an stresses compassion, benevolence, justice and wisdom. That compassion and mercy are central themes in Islam should be self-evident when almost every chapter of the Qur'an begins with: In the Name of God, The Most Compassionate, The Most Merciful.

In a famous saying of Muhammad, may God bless him and grant him peace, he says: 'The merciful are shown mercy by the Merciful one. Show mercy to those on earth and you will be shown mercy by the One in Heaven.' The Qur'an declares that Muhammad was sent as a Mercy to the worlds (21:107), something to which he himself testified when he refused to curse a warring tribe: 'I have not been sent to curse, but as a summoner and as a mercy'. Indeed, such is the centrality of mercy and compassion in Islam, that the aforementioned tradition is the first tradition of Muhammad, may God bless him and grant him peace, that is taught to the student of Sacred Law. Muslim scholars have said that in every matter, Muslims should be just, merciful and wise – anything that is lacking in any one of these principles cannot be said to be derived from Sacred Law.

Compassion in Islam is not restricted to Muslims only, but it also requires sensitivity to the suffering of others. In a tradition, the Messenger of God, may God bless him and grant him peace, declared that 'people are God's children and those dearest to God are the ones who treat His children kindly.'[12] A Muslim cannot be considered to be compassionate while there is suffering and injustice around them. It is for this reason, that Islam requires the community of believers to be one in which caring for your neighbours is an integral component of belief. The concern for your neighbour (irrespective of whether they are Muslim or not) is so crucial, that the Prophet, may God bless him and grant him peace, used to say that even if one person remains hungry in a particular area, no angel will descend in that area until that hungry person is fed.[13]

TIME to REFLECT

We cannot blame religion for the errors of those who use its name or symbols to justify their heinous actions. As Harun Yahya illustrates throughout this book, all religions, have had their share of people who claimed to be strict adherents of their tradition, but who actually grossly misinterpreted their sacred texts to suit their own agendas.

All true religious traditions condemn categorically any sort of act of aggression, and certainly any act of terror. Religion cannot be blamed, but the insanity and hate that drives people to commit such atrocities can be. It would not suffice to leave the condemnation there, it is up to us to seek out the root from which this hate pours forth; what are the causes of their grievances, turmoil, anger, bitterness, frustrations, hopelessness and how can we help to eliminate them?[14] We will soon realise that the causes are not the doing of God or religion, but merely results of regimes that oppress and policies that kill and subvert. Now more than ever there is a need to investigate the link between terrorism and the support that continues for dictatorial regimes, particularly in the Muslim World.

It is not the case that the Muslim world hates the 'West' or indeed America. There are many Muslims living in the West and it would be hypocritical to denounce in a rhetoric of hate the very host country that has welcomed them. Most Muslims realise that there are many similarities extant in the West to Islamic precepts, such as freedom, tolerance, the right to education, and civil liberties. Graham E. Fuller, the former vice-chairman of the National Intelligence Council at the CIA, recently wrote in the L.A Times that: 'If you travel around the Muslim world, it quickly becomes evident that there is immense respect for a great variety of American values.'Rather, the frustration is vented on what is seen as double standards in government policies. People can enjoy such values in the West, but it appears that there has been a concerted effort to keep such values restricted 'fit for home consumption, but not for export.'[15]

The Muslims in the West are facing a defining moment. Muslims must recapture the true spirit of Islam, and reclaim it from those who have harmed its integrity and honour. As Tim Winter asserts'[M]ainstream Islam will be able to make the loud declaration in public that it already feels in its heart: that terrorists are not Muslims. Targeting civilians is a negation of every possible school of Sunni Islam.'[16]

Harun Yahya's elucidation is timely and much needed. It will, God willing, provide Muslims and non-Muslims alike with an essential understanding of the very heart of Islam, and what has been understood and practised by the vast majority of Muslims throughout history. This is orthodox, Sunni, mainstream Islam. He illustrates by using the core text of all Muslims – the Holy Qur'an, that true Islam cannot in any way, shape or form be associated with terrorism. It is in complete contradistinction to it, for without a doubt, Islam itself denounces Terrorism.

Aftab Ahmad Malik
Amal Press

The Mercy-giving will grant affection
to those who believe and perform
honourable deeds. (Qur'an, 19:96)

INTRODUCTION

As Muslims, we strongly condemn the terrorist attacks on two major cities of the United States of America on September 11, 2001, which caused the death and injury of thousands of innocent people, and we offer our condolences to the American nation. These attacks propelled the important issue of the true source of terrorism to the top of the world agenda. Thus, it has been announced to the entire world that Islam is a religion of peace and tolerance that summons individuals to compassion and justice. Many world leaders, leading media organisations, television and radio stations said that true Islam forbids violence, and encourages

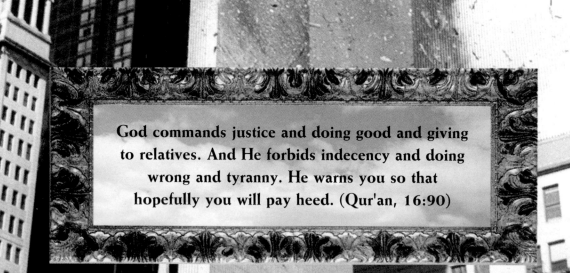

God commands justice and doing good and giving to relatives. And He forbids indecency and doing wrong and tyranny. He warns you so that hopefully you will pay heed. (Qur'an, 16:90)

peace between people and between nations. The Western circles that have come to a full grasp of the religion of Islam and are well-informed about Islam as commanded by God in the Qur'an noted clearly that the words "Islam" and "terror" cannot stand side by side, and that no divine religion permits violence.

This book maintains that the source of the terror that we condemn is definitely not from a divine religion, and that there is no room for terrorism in Islam. This is made clear in the Qur'an, the main source of Islam, and in the practices of all true Muslim rulers, the Prophet Muhammad being the foremost of them. This book reveals, in the light of the verses of the Qur'an and with examples from history, that Islam forbids terrorism and aims to bring peace and security to the world.

As is known, for centuries, various acts of terrorism have been carried out in different parts of the world by different groups for a variety of purposes. Sometimes a communist organisation, sometimes a fascist group, and sometimes radical and separatist factions assume responsibility for these acts. While countries like America often became the target of attacks by racist and marginal terrorist groups, the European countries have been centre stage for violent acts carried out by terrorist groups. 17 November in Greece, RAF (Red Army Faction) and Neo-Nazis in Germany, ETA in Spain, Red Brigades in Italy and many other organisations seek to make their voices heard through terror and violence by killing innocent and defenceless people. The nature of terrorism changes with changing world conditions and increases its impact and power with the new means made possible by developing technology. In particular, mass communication tools such as the Internet extend the scope and influence of the terrorist activities considerably.

Besides the Western organisations, there are also other terror organisations of Middle East origin. Terrorist attacks are carried out by these groups in all corners of the world. Sadly, the fact that the perpetrators of various terrorist acts carry Christian, Muslim or Jewish identities cause some people to put forward claims which do not concur with divine religions. The truth is that even if terrorists have Muslim identities, the terror they perpetrate cannot be labelled "Islamic terror", just as it could not be called "Jewish terror" if the perpetrators were Jews or "Christian terror" if they were Christians. That

If one is looking for the cause of an act of terrorism, one must look for its source in anti-religious ideologies. Religion enjoins love, compassion, forgiveness, peace and living according to high moral standards. Terrorism, on the other hand, is on the side of cruelty and violence, causing pain, bloodshed and committing murder.

is because, as will be examined in the following pages, **murdering innocent people in the name of a divine religion is unacceptable.** We need to keep in mind that, among those who were killed in New York and Washington, there were people who loved the Prophet Jesus (Christians), the

Prophet Moses (Jews) and the Prophet Muhammad (Muslims). Unless forgiven by God, murdering innocent people is a great sin that leads to torment in Hell. No one who is religious and fears God would do such a thing.

The aggressors can commit such violence only with the intention of attacking religion itself. It may well be that those who carried out this violence did so to present religion as evil in the eyes of people, to divorce people from religion and to generate hatred towards those who are religiously inclined. Consequently, every attack on American citizens or other innocent people having a religious facade is actually an attack made against religion.

Religion commands love, mercy and peace. Terror, on the other hand, is the opposite of religion; it is cruel, merciless and demands bloodshed and misery. This being the case, the origins of a terrorist act should be sought in disbelief rather than in religion. People with a fascist, communist, racist or materialist outlook on life should be suspected as potential perpetrators. The name or the identity of the triggerman is not important. If he can kill innocent people without blinking an eye, then he is a nonbeliever, not a believer. He is a murderer with no fear of God, whose main ambition is to shed blood and to cause harm. For this reason, "Islamic terror" is an erroneous concept which contradicts the message of Islam. The religion of Islam can by no means countenance terrorism. On the contrary, **terror (i.e. murder of innocent people) in Islam is a great sin, and Muslims are responsible for preventing these acts and bringing peace and justice to the world.**

Eat and drink of God's provision
and do not go about the earth
corrupting it. (Qur'an, 2:60)

ISLAMIC MORALITY: THE SOURCE OF PEACE AND SECURITY

Some of those who say that something is done in the name of religion may, in fact, misunderstand that religion and as a result, practice it wrongly. For that reason, it would be wrong to form ideas about that religion by taking these people as an example. The best way of understanding a religion is to study its divine source.

Islam's divine source is the Qur'an, which is based on concepts of morality, love, compassion, humility, sacrifice, tolerance and peace. A Muslim who lives by those precepts in its true sense will be most polite, careful of thought, modest, just, trustworthy and easy to get on with. He will spread love, respect, harmony and the joy of living all around him.

Islam is the Religion of Peace

Terror, in its broadest sense, is violence committed against non-military targets for political purposes. To put it another way, targets of terror are entirely innocent civilians whose only crime, in the eyes of terrorists, is to represent "the other side".

For this reason, terror means subjecting innocent people to violence, which is an act bereft of any moral justification. This, as in the case of murders

Terrorists aim to create a world of violence, conflict, chaos, and fear.

A society in which Islamic moral values are truly honoured is a society characterised by peace, forgiveness, love, compassion and mutual support and joy.

committed by Hitler or Stalin, is a crime committed against mankind.

The Qur'an is a Book revealed to people as a guide to the true path and in this Book, God commands man to adopt good morals. This morality is based upon concepts such as love, compassion, tolerance and mercy. The word "Islam" is derived from the word meaning "peace" in Arabic. Islam is a religion revealed to mankind with the intention of presenting a peaceful life through which the infinite compassion and mercy of God manifest on earth. God calls all people to Islamic morals through which compassion, mercy, peace and tolerance can be experienced all over the world. In Sura Baqara, verse 208, God addresses believers as follows:

O You who believe! Enter absolutely into peace (Islam). Do not follow in the footsteps of Satan. He is an outright enemy to you.

As the verse makes clear, security can only be ensured by "entering into Islam", that is, living by the values of the Qur'an. The values of the Qur'an hold a Muslim responsible for treating all people, whether Muslim or non-Muslim, kindly and justly, protecting the needy and the innocent and **"preventing the**

dissemination of mischief". Mischief comprises all forms of anarchy and terror that remove security, comfort and peace. As God says in a verse, **"God does not love corruption"**. (Qur'an, 2:205)

Murdering a person for no reason is one of the most obvious examples of mischief. God repeats in the Qur'an a command He formerly revealed to Jews in the Old Testament thus:

> **...if someone kills another person – unless it is in retaliation for someone else or for causing corruption in the earth – it is as if he had murdered all mankind. And if anyone gives life to another person, it is as if he had given life to all mankind... (Qur'an, 5:32)**

As the verse suggests, a person who kills even a single man, "unless it is in retaliation for someone else or for causing corruption in the earth", commits a crime as if he had murdered all mankind.

This being the case, it is obvious what great sins are the murders, massacres and attacks, popularly known as "suicide attacks", committed by terrorists. God informs us how this cruel face of terrorism will be punished in the hereafter in the following verse:

In Sura Ma'ida, verse 32, God says that if anyone kills someone unjustly, it is as if he had murdered all mankind. To murder even one person is totally opposed to the moral teaching of the Qur'an.

There are only grounds against those who wrong people and act as tyrants in the earth without any right to do so. Such people will have a painful punishment. (Qur'an, 42:42)

All these reveal that organising acts of terror against innocent people is utterly against Islam and it is unlikely that any Muslim could ever commit such crimes. On the contrary, Muslims are responsible for stopping these people, removing "mischief on earth" and bringing peace and security to all people all over the world. Islam cannot be reconciled with terror. Just the contrary, it should be the solution to and the path to the prevention of terror.

God has Condemned Wickedness

God has commanded people to avoid committing evil: oppression, cruelty, murder and bloodshed are all forbidden. He describes those who fail to obey this command as **"following in Satan's footsteps"** and adopting a posture that is openly revealed to be sinful in the Qur'an. A few of the many verses on this matter in the Qur'an read:

But as for those who break God's contract after it has been agreed and sever what God has commanded to be joined, and cause corruption in the earth, the curse will be upon them. They will have the Evil Abode. (Qur'an, 13:25)

Eat and drink of God's provision and <u>do not go about the earth corrupting it.</u> (Qur'an, 2:60)

<u>Do not corrupt the earth</u> after it has been put right. Call on Him fearfully and eagerly. God's mercy is close to the good-doers. (Qur'an, 7:56)

Those who think that they will be successful by causing wickedness, upheaval and oppression, and by killing innocent people are committing a great error. God has forbidden all acts of wickedness involving terrorism and violence, condemned those who engage in such acts and said **"God does not uphold the works of those who cause mischief."** in one of His verses. (Qur'an, 10:81)

In the present age, however, acts of terrorism, genocide and massacres

There are apparently many reasons for the acts of terror which have now claimed perhaps hundreds of thousands of lives. Those who perpetrate such acts have no fear of God. To them, the morality enjoined by religion is completely alien.

occur all over the world. Innocent people are being savagely killed, and countries where communities are being brought to hate each other for artificial reasons are drowning in blood. These horrors in countries with different histories, cultures and social structures may have causes and sources peculiar to each. However, it is evident that the fundamental cause is a moving away from morality based on love, respect and tolerance that religion brings with it. As a result of lack of religion, communities emerge that have no fear of God and believe that they will not be called to account in the hereafter. Since they believe that, "I will not have to account for my actions to anyone," they can easily act with no compassion, morality or conscience.

The existence of hypocrites who emerge in the name of God and religion, but actually organise themselves to commit wickedness condemned by God, is indicated in the Qur'an. One verse talks about a gang of nine men who planned to murder the Prophet by swearing in the name of God:

There was a gang of nine men in the city causing corruption in the land and not putting things right. They said, "Let us make an oath to one another by God that we will fall on him and his family in the night and then say to his protector, We did not witness the destruction of his family and we are telling the truth." They hatched a plot and We hatched a plot while they were not aware. (Qur'an, 27:48-50)

As this incident described in the Qur'an reveals, the fact that people do things "in the name of God" or even swear in His name, in other words that they use the kind of language designed to show themselves as very religious, does not mean that what they do is in conformity with religion. On the contrary, what they do can be quite against the will of God and the morality of religion. The truth of the matter lies in their actions. If their actions are **"causing corruption and not putting things right"**, as the verse reveals, then you can be sure that these people cannot be truly religious, and that their aim is not to serve religion.

It is quite impossible for someone who fears God and has grasped the true morality of Islam to support violence or wickedness, or to take part in such actions. That is why Islam is the true solution to terrorism. When the sublime morality of the Qur'an is explained, it will be impossible for people to connect true Islam with those who support or join groups that aim at hatred, war and chaos. That is because God has forbidden wickedness:

Whenever he holds the upperhand, he goes about the earth corrupting it, destroying (people's) crops and breeding stock. God does not love corruption. When he is told to have fear of God, he is seized by pride which drives him to wrongdoing. Hell will be enough for him! What an evil resting-place. (Qur'an, 2:205-206)

As can be seen from the above verses, it is out of the question for someone who fears God to turn a blind eye to even the smallest action that might harm mankind. Someone who does not believe in God and the hereafter, however, can easily do all kinds of evil, since he thinks he will not have to account to anyone.

The first thing that needs to be done to rid the world of the present-day

The Responsibility of Believers

Those who have no concern for events unless they directly affect them are bereft of the insight that espouses unselfishness, brotherhood, friendship, honesty and the service that religion bestows upon people. Throughout their lives, such people try to satisfy their own egos by merely wasting their means, totally unaware of the threats humanity faces. In the Qur'an however, God praises the morals of those who strive to bring good to their surroundings; those who are concerned about the events that take place around them and who call people to the right way. In a verse from the Qur'an, a metaphor is given for those who offer no good to others and those who always act on the path of goodness:

God makes another metaphor: two men, one of them deaf and dumb, unable to do anything, a burden on his master, no matter where he directs him he brings no good, is he the same as someone who commands justice and is on a straight path? (Qur'an, 16:76)

As the verse points out, it is obvious that those who are "on a straight path", are those who are devoted to their religion; fear and heed God, hold spiritual values in high regard, and are filled with eagerness to serve people. In general, such people are there to serve humanity and bring with them great benefits to mankind. For this reason, it is very important for people to learn about the true religion and live by the morals explained by the Qur'an – the final Revelation from God. In the Qur'an, God defines those people who live by such high morals:

Those who, if We establish them firmly on the earth, will keep up prayer and pay the welfare due, and command what is right and forbid what is wrong. The end result of all affairs is with God. (Qur'an, 22:41)

scourge of terrorism is to use education to do away with deviant irreligious beliefs that are put forward in the name of religion, and to teach people true Qur'anic morality and to fear God.

God Commands Us to Do Good Deeds

A Muslim is someone who abides by the commands of God, tries scrupulously to live by Qur'anic morality, peace and harmony, which make the world a more beautiful place and lead it to progress. His aim is to lead people to beauty, goodness and well-being. The Qur'an says:

Those who threaten the lives of civilians, and especially those of children, must ask themselves: What crime did these children commit? Is committing cruel acts against innocent people something that will go unaccounted for in the presence of God?

... And do good as God has been good to you. And do not seek to cause corruption in the earth. God does not love corrupters. (Qur'an, 28:77)

Someone who adopts the Islamic faith wishes to earn God's pleasure and compassion and to enter heaven. He has to make strenuous efforts to do this, and to adopt a morality acceptable to God while he is in this world. The clearest manifestations of this morality are compassion, pity, justice, honesty, forgiveness, humility, sacrifice and patience. The believer will behave well towards people, try to perform good deeds and spread goodness. In His verses, God commands:

We did not create the heavens and earth and everything between them, except with truth. The Hour is certainly coming, so forgive [men's failings] with fair forbearance. (Qur'an, 15:85)

... Be good to your parents and relatives and to orphans and the very poor, and to neighbours who are related to you and neighbours who are not related to you, and to companions and travellers and your slaves. God does not love anyone vain or boastful. (Qur'an, 4:36)

... Help one another in benevolence and piety. Do not help each other to

In the moral teachings of Islam, the most important qualities are love, compassion, mutual support, self-sacrifice, tolerance and forgiveness. In a society where this morality is lived as it should be, it is impossible to find the foundations of violence and conflict.

wrongdoing and enmity. And fear God. God is severe in retribution. (Qur'an, 5:2)

As the verses have made clear, God wishes those who believe in Him to behave well towards people, to cooperate with each other when it comes to goodness, and to avoid wickedness. In Sura Anam, verse 160, God promises that **"anyone who comes with a fine deed will have ten more like it. But those who produce a bad action will only be repaid with its equivalent and they will not be wronged."**

In His book, God describes Himself as He who knows **"the secrets of men's hearts"**, and warns people to **"avoid all kinds of evil."** A Muslim therefore, which means **"one who surrenders himself to God"** must evidently be someone who does his best to fight terrorism.

A Muslim does not remain indifferent to what goes on around him, and never adopts the mentality that nothing matters as long as it does not harm him. That is because he has surrendered himself to God. He is His representative, and an ambassador of good. He cannot, therefore, remain indifferent in the face of cruelty and terrorism. In fact, the Muslim is the greatest enemy of terrorism, which kills people who have done no wrong. Islam is against all forms of terrorism, and tries to prevent it right from the beginning, in other words on the level of ideas. It demands peace between people and for justice to prevail, and commands people to avoid discord, conflict and wickedness.

God Commands Us to Be Just

The true justice described in the Qur'an commands man to behave justly, making no discrimination between people, to protect peoples' rights, not to permit violence no matter what the circumstances, to side with the oppressed against the oppressor and to help the needy. This justice calls for the rights of both parties to be protected when reaching a decision in a dispute, assessing all aspects of an incident, setting aside all prejudices, being objective, honest, tolerant, merciful and compassionate. For instance, someone who cannot assess events in a moderate way, and who is swayed by his emotions and feelings, will fail to arrive at sound decisions and will remain under the influence of those feelings. However, someone who rules with justice needs to set all his personal feelings and views aside. He needs to treat all parties with justice when they ask for help, to side with what is right under all circumstances, and not to diverge from the path of honesty and truthfulness. A person should incorporate the values of the Qur'an into his soul in such a way that he may be able to consider other parties' interests before his own and maintain justice, even if this harms his own interests.

God commands the following in Sura Ma'ida, verse 42: **"... if you do judge, judge between them justly."** In Sura Nisa, God commands believers to act justly even it is against themselves:

> **O You who believe! Be upholders of justice, bearing witness for God alone, even against yourselves or your parents and relatives. Whether they are rich or poor, God is well able to look after them. Do not follow your own desires and deviate from the truth. If you twist or turn away, God is aware of what you do. (Qur'an, 4:135)**

In the Qur'an, God gives a detailed description of justice and informs believers of the attitude they have to adopt in the face of incidents they encounter and of the ways to exercise justice. Such guidance is a great comfort to believers and a mercy from God. For this reason, those who believe are responsible for exercising justice in an undivided manner both to earn God's approval and to lead their lives in peace and security.

The justice God commands in the Qur'an is the justice that is exercised equally among all people, with no consideration of language, race, or ethnicity. The justice in the Qur'anic sense does not vary according to place, time and people. In our day, too, there are people being subjected to cruel and unjust treatment because of the colour of their skin or their race in all corners of the world.

However, God informs us in the Qur'an that the purpose in the creation of different tribes and peoples is **"that they should come to know each other"**. Different nations or peoples, all of whom are the servants of God, should get to know one another, that is, learn about their different cultures, languages, traditions and abilities. In brief, the purpose of the creation of different races and nations is not conflict and war but cultural richness. Such variation is a

bounty of God's creation. The fact that someone is taller than someone else or that his skin is yellow or white neither makes him superior to others nor is it something to feel ashamed of. Every trait a person has is a result of God's purposeful creation, but in the sight of God, these variations have no ultimate importance. A believer knows that someone attains superiority only by having fear of God and in the strength of his faith in God. This fact is related in the following verse:

> **O Mankind! We created you from a male and female, and made you into peoples and tribes so that you might come to know each other. The noblest among you in God's sight is that one of you who best performs his duty. God is All-Knowing, All-Aware. (Qur'an, 49:13)**

As God informs us in the verse, the understanding of justice recommended by Him calls for equal, tolerant and peaceable treatment of everyone, with no discrimination between them.

Hatred Felt Towards a Community Does Not Prevent Believers From Exercising Justice

Hatred and anger are the major sources of evil, and are likely to prevent people from making just decisions, thinking soundly and conducting themselves rationally. People can readily inflict all kinds of injustice on people for whom they feel enmity. They may accuse these people of acts they have never committed, or bear false witness against them although their innocence is known to them. On account of such enmity, people may be subjected to unbearable oppression. Some people avoid bearing witness in favour of people they disagree with, although they know they are innocent, and they keep evidence which would reveal their innocence hidden. Furthermore, they take pleasure in the misery these people face, their encounters with injustice or great suffering. Their greatest worry, on the other hand, is that justice should be done and these peoples' innocence proved.

For these reasons, it is very hard for people in corrupt societies to trust one another. People worry that they can fall victim to someone else at any time. Having lost mutual trust, they also lose their human feelings such as tolerance, compassion, brotherhood and co-operation, and start hating one another.

However, the feelings someone holds in his heart towards a person or community should never influence a believer's decisions. No matter how immoral or hostile the person he is considering may be, the believer sets all these feelings aside and acts and makes his decisions justly and recommends that which is just. His feelings towards that person cast no shadow over his wisdom and conscience. His conscience always inspires him to comply with God's commands and advice, and never to abandon good manners, because this is a command God gives in the Qur'an. In Sura Ma'ida, it is related as follows:

> **O You who believe! Show integrity for the sake of God, bearing witness with justice. Do not let hatred for a people incite you into not being just. Be just. That is closer to faith. Heed God (alone). God is aware of what you do. (Qur'an, 5:8)**

As is related in the verse, displaying a just attitude is what most complies

If your Lord had willed, all the people on the earth would have believed. Do you think you can force people to be believers? (Qur'an, 10:99)

with having fear of God. A person of faith knows that he will attain the pleasure of God only when he acts justly. Every person who witnesses his or her good manners will trust this person, feel comfortable in their presence and trust them with any responsibility or task. Such people are treated with respect even by their enemies. Their attitude may even lead some people to have faith in God.

Islam Defends Freedom of Thought

Islam is a religion which provides and guarantees freedom of ideas, thought and life. It has issued commands to prevent and forbid tension, disputes, slander and even negative thinking among people. In the same way that it is determinedly opposed to terrorism and all acts of violence, it has also forbidden even the slightest ideological pressure to be put on them:

There is no compulsion in religion. True guidance has become clearly distinct from error. (Qur'an, 2:256)

So remind them! You are only a reminder. You are not in control of them. (Qur'an, 88:21-22)

Forcing people to believe in a religion or to adopt its forms of belief is completely contrary to the essence and spirit of Islam. According to Islam, true faith is only possible with free will and freedom of conscience. Of course,

No matter what another person's religion or belief may be, be they Jew, Christian, Buddhist or Hindu, Muslims are called on in the Qur'an to be tolerant, forgiving, and to act justly and humanely towards them.

Muslims can advise and encourage each other about the features of Qur'anic morality. All believers are charged with explaining Qur'anic morality to people in the nicest manner possible. They will explain the beauties of religion in the light of the verse, **"Call to the way of your Lord with wisdom and fair admonition..."** (Qur'an, 16:125), however, they must also bear in mind the verse, **"You are not responsible for their guidance, but God guides whoever He wills."** (Qur'an, 2:272)

They will never resort to compulsion, nor any kind of physical or psychological pressure. Neither will they use any worldly privilege to turn someone towards religion. When they receive a negative response to what they say, Muslims will reply along the lines of: **"To you your religion, and to me, mine"** (Qur'an, 109:6)

The world we live in contains societies with all kinds of beliefs: Christian, Jewish, Buddhist, Hindu, atheist, deist and even pagan. Muslims living in such a world must be tolerant of all beliefs they come up against, no matter what they may be, and behave forgivingly, justly and humanely. This responsibility placed on believers is to invite people to the beauty of the religion of God by means of peace and tolerance. The decision whether or not to implement these truths, whether or not to believe, lies with the other party. Forcing that person to believe, or trying to impose anything on him, is a violation of Qur'anic morality. In fact, God issues a reminder to believers in the Qur'an:

> **If your Lord had willed, all the people on the earth would have believed. Do you think you can force people to be believers? (Qur'an, 10:99)**

> **We know best what they say and you [O Muhammad] are not a compeller over them. But warn by the Qur'an whoever fears My warning. (Qur'an, 50:45)**

A model of society in which people are forced to worship is completely contradictory to Islam. **Belief and worship are only of any value when they are directed to God by the free will of the individual**. If a system imposes belief and worship on people, then they will become religious out of fear of that system. From the religious point of view, what really counts is that religion should be lived for God's good pleasure in an environment where peoples' consciences are totally free.

The history of Islam is full of the tolerant practices of Muslim rulers who have respected all religions and built religious freedom with their own hands. For example, Thomas Arnold, a British missionary employed in the service of the Indian government, describes that Islam favours freedom in these words:

> But of any organised attempt to force the acceptance of Islam on the non-Muslim population, or of any systematic persecution intended to stamp

In 1492, the Jews who refused to convert were exiled from Spain by King Ferdinand and Queen Isabella (above). The Jews were accepted by the Ottoman Empire, a haven of Islamic justice and tolerance.

out the Christian religion, we hear nothing. Had the caliphs chosen to adopt either course of action, they might have swept away Christianity as easily as Ferdinand and Isabella drove Islam out of Spain, or Louis XIV made Protestantism penal in France, or the Jews were kept out of England for 350 years. The Eastern Churches in Asia were entirely cut off from communion with the rest of Christendom, throughout which no one would have been found to lift a finger on their behalf, as heretical communions. So that the very survival of these Churches to the present day is a strong proof of the generally tolerant attitude of the Muhammadan governments towards them.[1]

God Forbids the Murder of Innocent People

Killing a person for no reason is one of the greatest sins related in the Qur'an:

> **... if someone kills another person – unless it is in retaliation for someone else or for causing corruption in the earth – it is as if he had murdered all mankind. And if anyone gives life to another person, it is as if he had given life to all mankind. Our Messengers came to them with Clear Signs, but even after that many of them committed outrages in the earth. (Qur'an, 5:32)**

> **..those who do not call on any other deity together with God and do not kill anyone God has made inviolate, except with the right to do so, and do not fornicate; anyone who does that will receive an evil punishment. (Qur'an, 25:68)**

As the verse suggests, a person who kills innocent people for no reason is threatened with a great torment. God informs us that killing even a single person is as evil as murdering all mankind on earth. A person who observes God's limits can do no harm to a single human, let alone massacre thousands of innocent people. Those who assume that they can avoid justice and thus punishment in this world will never succeed, for they will have to give an account of their deeds in the presence of God. That is why believers, who know that they will give an account of their deeds after death, are very meticulous to observe God's limits.

God Commands the Faithful to be Compassionate and Merciful

Islamic morality is described in one verse as:

Then to be one of those who have faith and urge each other to steadfastness and urge each other to compassion. Those are the Companions of the Right. (Qur'an, 90:17-18)

As we have seen in this verse, one of the most important features of the morality that will lead believers to salvation on the Day of Judgement and to enter into paradise is "**being one of those who urges each other to compassion**".

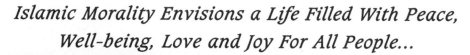

Islamic Morality Envisions a Life Filled With Peace, Well-being, Love and Joy For All People...

The true source of compassion is love of God. A person's love of God gives rise to his feeling love for the things He has created. Someone who loves God feels a direct link and closeness to the things He has created. This strong love and closeness he feels for the Lord, who created him and all mankind, leads him to display a pleasing morality, as commanded in the Qur'an. True compassion emerges as he lives by this morality. This model of morality, full of love, compassion and sacrifice, is described in these verses:

> **Those of you possessing affluence and ample wealth should not make oaths that they will not give to their relatives and the very poor and those who have made emigration in the way of God. They should rather pardon and overlook. Would you not love God to forgive you? God is Ever-Forgiving, Most Merciful. (Qur'an, 24:22)**

...While terrorism longs for a society where violence, fear, anxiety and chaos reign.

Those who were already settled in the abode and in faith before they came, love those who have migrated to them and do not find in their hearts any need for what they have been given and prefer them to themselves even if they themselves are needy. It is the people who are safe-guarded from the avarice of their own selves who are successful. (Qur'an, 59:9)

... those who have given refuge and help, they are the true believers. They will have forgiveness and generous provision. (Qur'an, 8:74)

Be good to your parents and relatives and to orphans and the very poor, and to neighbours who are related to you and neighbours who are not related to you, and to companions and travellers and your slaves. God does not love anyone vain or boastful. (Qur'an, 4:36)

Charity (zakat) is for: the poor, the destitute, those who collect it, reconciling people's hearts, freeing slaves, those in debt, spending in the Way of God, and travellers. It is a legal obligation from God. God is All-Knowing, All-Wise. (Qur'an, 9:60)

This high level of morality that is demanded from believers, described in the Qur'an, stems from their deep love of God. Thanks to their devotion to Him, they scrupulously abide by the morality revealed by Him in the Qur'an. Believers never try to make people feel indebted because of the compassion they demonstrate and the help they offer people, and do not even expect to be thanked. Their true aim is to try to gain God's good pleasure by means of the morality they exhibit, because they know that they will be called to account for that morality on the Day of Judgement. In the Qur'an, God has expressly revealed that hell will be the outcome for those who knowingly refuse to live by the morality of the Qur'an:

"What has brought you into hell-fire?" They will say, "We were not among those who prayed and we did not feed the poor." (Qur'an, 74:42-44)

Seize him and bind him, and then expose him to hell-fire, then fasten him with a chain seventy cubits long! For he did not believe in God Almighty, nor did he urge the feeding of the poor. (Qur'an, 69:30-34)

Islamic morality commands Muslims to protect the rights of orphans and those in poverty and need, to mutually support one another, and to be well-disposed towards one another.

Have you seen him who denies the religion? He is the one who harshly rebuffs the orphan and does not urge the feeding of the poor. (Qur'an, 107:1-3)

...nor do you urge the feeding of the poor (Qur'an, 89:18)

As we have seen in these verses, the Muslim described in the Qur'an possesses a most loving and compassionate nature. Nobody who possesses this morality can of course consent to terrorism or acts of violence directed at innocent people. Terrorists' characters are the exact opposite of Qur'anic morality. A terrorist is a ruthless person who looks with hatred on the world, and wants to kill, destroy and shed blood.

A Muslim raised in the morality as revealed by the Qur'an, however, approaches everyone with the love expected by Islam, respects ideas of all kinds, always tries to bring harmony where there is discord, lower tensions, embrace all sides and behave with moderation. Societies consisting of people like this will be ruled by a more developed civilisation, and enjoy greater social morality, harmony, justice and plenty than can be seen in even the most modern nations today.

God has Commanded Forgiveness and Tolerance

The concept of forgiveness and tolerance, described in the words, **"Make allowances for people"** (Qur'an, 7:199) is one of the most fundamental tenets of Islam.

When we look at the history of Islam, the way that Muslims have translated this important feature of Qur'anic morality into the life of society can be seen quite clearly. As we shall be considering in later parts of the book, Muslims have always brought with them an atmosphere of freedom and tolerance wherever they have gone. They have enabled people whose religions, languages and cultures are completely different from one another to live together in peace and harmony under one roof, and provided peace and harmony for its own members. One of the most important reasons for the centuries-long existence of the Ottoman Empire, which spread over an enormous region, was the atmosphere of tolerance and understanding that Islam brought with it. Muslims, who have been known for their tolerant and loving natures for centuries, have always been the most compassionate and

In societies where Islamic morality is followed, churches, mosques and synagogues co-exist peacefully. This view of three sanctuaries in an institution for the homeless shows the tolerance, justice and striving for peace inculcated by the teaching of Islamic morality.

just of people. Within this multi-national structure, all ethnic groups have been free to live according to their own religions, and their own rules.

True tolerance can only bring peace and well-being to the world when implemented along the lines set out in the Qur'an. Attention is drawn to this fact in a verse which reads: **"A good action and a bad action are not the same. Repel the bad with something better and, if there is enmity between you and someone else, he will be like a bosom friend."** (Qur'an, 41:34)

In the verses of the Qur'an, God has always described forgiveness as a superior quality, and in one verse, He has given the good news that such behaviour will be rewarded: **"The repayment of a bad action is one equivalent to it. But if someone pardons and puts things right, his reward is with God. Certainly He does not love wrongdoers."** (Qur'an, 42:40) In another verse, He has described believers as: **"those who give in times of both ease and hardship, those who control their rage and pardon other people – God loves the good-doers"** (Qur'an, 3:134) God has revealed in the Qur'an that it is virtuous behaviour to forgive someone even if he has done wrong. One verse on the subject reads:

> **... You will never cease to come upon some act of treachery on their part, except for a few of them. Yet pardon them, and overlook. God loves good-doers. (Qur'an, 5:13)**

All of this shows that the morality that Islam recommends to mankind brings to the world the virtues of peace, harmony and justice. The barbarism known as terrorism, that is so preoccupying the world at present, is the work of ignorant and fanatical people, completely estranged from Qur'anic morality, and who have absolutely nothing to do with religion. The solution to these people and groups who try to carry out their savagery under the mask of religion is the teaching of true Qur'anic morality. In other words, Islam and Qur'anic morality are solutions to the scourge of terrorism, not supporters of it.

...God is All-Gentle, Most Merciful to mankind. (Qur'an, 2:143)

WAR IN THE QUR'AN

According to the Qur'an, war represents an "unwanted obligation" which has to be carried out with strict observance of particular humane and moral guidelines and which must not be resorted to except when it is absolutely inevitable.

In one Qur'anic verse, it is explained that those who start wars are the disbelievers and that God does not approve of wars:

...Each time they kindle the fire of war, God extinguishes it. They rush about the earth corrupting it. God does not love corrupters.

(Qur'an, 5:64)

In the case of a conflict, before engaging in a war, believers must wait until fighting becomes compulsory. Believers are allowed to fight only when the other party attacks and no other alternative except war remains:

But if they cease (fighting), God is Ever-Forgiving, Most Merciful. (Qur'an, 2:192)

A closer examination of the Prophet Muhammad's life reveals that war was a method resorted for defensive purposes only in unavoidable situations.

The revelation of the Qur'an to the Prophet Muhammad continued for a period of 23 years. During the first 13 years of this period, Muslims lived as a minority under a pagan order in Mecca and faced much oppression. Many Muslims were harassed, abused, tortured, and even murdered, their houses and possessions plundered. Despite this, however, Muslims led their lives without resorting to violence and always called the pagans to peace.

When the oppression of the pagans escalated unbearably, the Muslims emigrated to the town of Yathrib, which was later to be renamed Madinah, where they could establish their own order in a freer and more friendly environment. Even establishing their own system did not prompt them to take up weapons against the aggressive pagans of Mecca. Only after the following

A view of present-day Madinah, the city to which the Prophet Muhammad and the Muslims emigrated and established their own polity.

revelation, the Prophet commanded his people to prepare for war:

> **Permission to fight is given to those who are fought against because they have been wronged – truly God has the power to come to their support – those who were expelled from their homes without any right, merely for saying, "Our Lord is God"... (Qur'an, 22:39-40)**

In brief, Muslims were allowed to wage war only because they were oppressed and subjected to violence. To put it in another way, God granted permission for war only for defensive purposes. In other verses, Muslims are warned against the use of unnecessary provocation or violence:

> **Fight in the Way of God against those who fight you, but do not go beyond the limits. God does not love those who go beyond the limits. (Qur'an, 2:190)**

After the revelation of these verses, several wars occurred between the Muslims and the pagan Arabs. In none of these wars, however, were the Muslims the inciting party. Furthermore, the Prophet Muhammad established a secure and peaceful social environment for Muslims and pagans alike by signing the peace agreement of Hudaybiya which conceded to the pagans most of their requests. The party who violated the terms of the agreement and started hostilities once again were the pagans. With rapid conversions into Islam, the Islamic armies mustered a great force against the pagan Arabs. However, Muhammad conquered Mecca without bloodshed and in a spirit of tolerance. If he wished, Muhammad could have taken revenge on pagan leaders in the city. Yet, he did not do harm to any one of them, forgave them and treated them with the utmost tolerance. In the words of John Esposito, a Western expert on Islam, "eschewing vengeance and the plunder of conquest, the Prophet instead accepted a settlement, granting amnesty rather than wielding the sword toward his former enemies." [2]

Pagans, who would later convert to Islam of their own free will, could not help admiring such nobility of character in the Prophet.

Not only during Mecca's conquest, but also in the course of all the battles and conquests made in the time of the Prophet Muhammad, the rights of innocent and defenceless people were meticulously protected. The Prophet

Muhammad reminded believers numerous times about this subject and by his own practice became a role model for others to follow. Indeed, he addressed believers who were about to go to war in the following terms: **"Go to war in adherence to the religion of God. Never touch the elderly, women or children. Always improve their situation and be kind to them. God loves those who are sincere."**[3] The Messenger of God also clarified the attitude Muslims must adopt even when they are in the middle of a raging battle:

> Do not kill children. Avoid touching people who devote themselves to worship in churches! Never murder women and the elderly. Do not set trees on fire or cut them down. Never destroy houses![4]

The Islamic principles God proclaims in the Qur'an account for this

The Ka'aba, to which almost two million Muslims come every year from the four corners of the world, is a symbol of the peace and tolerance that are an integral part of Islamic teaching.

peaceful and temperate policy of the Prophet Muhammad. In the Qur'an, God commands believers to treat the non-Muslims kindly and justly:

> God does not forbid you from being good to those who have not fought you over religion or driven you from your homes, or from being just towards them. God loves those who are just. God merely forbids you from taking as friends those who have fought you over religion and

driven you from your homes and who supported your expulsion...
(Qur'an, 60:8-9)

The verses above clarify how Muslims should behave towards non-Muslims: A Muslim should treat all non-Muslims kindly and only avoid making friends with those who show enmity towards Islam. In a case where this enmity causes violent attacks against Muslims, that is, where they wage a war against them, then Muslims should respond to them justly by considering the humane dimensions of the situation. All forms of barbarism, unnecessary acts of violence and unjust aggression are forbidden by Islam. In another verse, God warns Muslims against this and explains that rage felt towards enemies should not cause them to fall into injustice:

> You who believe! Show integrity for the sake of God, bearing witness with justice. Do not let hatred for a people incite you into not being just. Be just. That is closer to heedfulness. Heed God (alone). God is aware of what you do. (Qur'an, 5:8)

The Meaning of the Concept of "Jihad"

Another concept that deserves clarification due in the context of our discussion is that of "jihad".

The exact meaning of "Jihad" is "effort". Thus, in Islam, "to carry out jihad" is "to show effort, to struggle". The Prophet Muhammad explained that "the greatest jihad is the one a person carries out against his lower soul". What is meant by "lower soul" here is selfish desires and ambitions.

Assessed from the Qur'anic point of view, the word "jihad" can also mean a struggle carried out on intellectual grounds against those who oppress people, treat them unjustly, subject them to torture and cruelty and violate legitimate human rights. The purpose of this struggle is to bring about justice, peace and equality.

Apart from these ideological and spiritual meanings, struggle in the physical sense is also considered as "jihad". However, as explained above, this has to be a struggle carried out solely for defensive purposes. The use of the concept of "jihad" for acts of aggression against innocent people, that is for terror, would be unjust and a great distortion of the true meaning of the term.

Killing Oneself (Committing Suicide)
is Forbidden in the Qur'an

Another important matter that arose in the wake of the latest terrorist assaults against the United States is that of suicide attacks. Some people who are ill-informed on Islam have made utterly erroneous statements to the effect that this religion of peace allows suicide attacks, whereas in Islam killing oneself and killing other people are both prohibited. In the words, "**Do not kill yourselves.**" (Qur'an, 4:29) God has declared suicide to be a sin. In Islam it is forbidden for anyone to kill himself or herself, for no matter what reason.

The Prophet reveals suicide to be a sin in a parable, when he says that those who commit suicide will be punished:

Indeed, whoever (intentionally) kills himself, then certainly he will be punished in the Fire of Hell, wherein he shall dwell forever.[5]

As this makes clear, committing suicide, and thus carrying out suicide attacks, and causing the deaths of thousands of innocent people while doing so, is a total violation of Islamic morality. God says in the Qur'an that it is a sin

One of the main purposes of terrorist bombings, arson attacks and other such vicious acts is to create fear, anxiety, insecurity and a sense of panic in people.

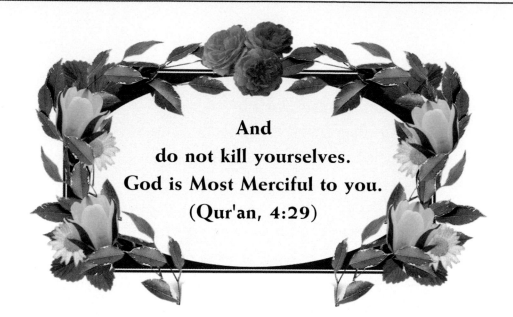

And
do not kill yourselves.
God is Most Merciful to you.
(Qur'an, 4:29)

to put an end to one's own life. For that reason, it is quite impossible for someone who believes in God and says he abides by the Qur'an to do such a thing. The only people who can do such things are those who have a very mistaken perception of religion, have no idea of true Qur'anic morality, fail to use their reason and conscience, are under the influence of atheist ideologies, and who have been brainwashed with feelings of hatred and revenge. Everybody must oppose such actions.

Compassion, Tolerance and Humanity in the History of Islam

To sum up the facts we have seen so far, we can say that the political doctrine of Islam (in other words, Islamic rules and principles regarding political matters) is exceedingly moderate and peace-loving. This truth is accepted by many non-Muslim historians and theologians. One of these is the British historian Karen Armstrong, a former nun and an expert on Middle East history. In her book *Holy War*, which examines the history of the three divine religions, she makes the following comments:

> ... The word 'Islam' comes from the same Arabic root as the word 'peace' and the Qur'an condemns war as an abnormal state of affairs opposed to God's will... Islam does not justify a total aggressive war of extermination... Islam recognises that war is inevitable and sometimes a positive duty in order to end oppression and suffering. **The Qur'an**

teaches that war must be limited and be conducted in as humane a way as possible. Mohammad had to fight not only the Meccans but also the Jewish tribes in the area and Christian tribes in Syria who planned on offensive against him in alliance with the Jews. Yet this did not make Mohammed denounce the People of the Book. His Muslims were forced to defend themselves but they were not fighting a 'holy war' against the religion of their enemies. When Mohammad sent his freedman Zaid against the Christians at the head of a Muslim army, he told them **to fight in the cause of God bravely but humanely.** They must not molest priests, monks and nuns nor the weak and helpless people who were unable to fight. There must be no massacre of civilians nor should they cut down a single tree nor pull down any building.[6]

After the death of the Prophet, the Caliphs who succeeded him were also very sensitive in exercising justice. In conquered countries, both the indigenous people and the newcomers led their lives in peace and security. Abu Bakr, the first Caliph, demanded his people adopt just and tolerant attitudes in these lands. All these attitudes were in compliance with the values of the Qur'an. Abu Bakr gave the following command to his army before the first Syrian expedition:

> Stop, O people, that I may give you ten rules to keep by heart: Do not commit treachery, nor depart from the right path. You must not mutilate, neither kill a child or aged man or woman. Do not destroy a palm tree, nor burn it with fire and do not cut any fruitful tree. You msut not slay any of the flock or herds or the camels, save for your subsistence. You are likely to pass by people who have devoted their lives to monastic services; leave them to that to which they have devoted their lives. You are likely, likewise, to find people who will present to you meals of many kinds. You may eat; but do no forget to mention the name of Allah.[7]

Umar ibn al-Khattab, who succeeded Abu Bakr, was famous for the way he exercised justice and made contracts with the indigenous people of the conquered countries. Each one of these contracts proved to be an example of tolerance and justice. For instance, in his declaration granting protection to Christians in Jerusalem and Lod, he ensured that churches would not be demolished and guaranteed that Muslims would not worship in churches in groups. Umar granted the same conditions to the Christians of Bethlehem. During the conquest of Medain, the declaration of protection given to the Nestorian Patriarch Isho'yab III (650 - 660 AD) again guaranteed that churches would not be demolished and that no building would be converted into a house or a mosque. The letter written by the patriarch to the bishop of Fars (Persia) after the conquest is most striking, in the sense that it depicts the tolerance and compassion shown by Muslim rulers to the Book of People in the words of a Christian:

> The Arabs to whom God has given at this time the government of the world... do not persecute the Christian religion. Indeed, they favour it, honour our priests and the saints of the Lord and confer benefits on churches and monasteries.[8]

All these are very important examples revealing the understanding of justice and tolerance of true believers. In a verse God commands the following:

God commands you to return to their owners the things you hold on trust and, when you judge between people, to judge with justice. How excellent is what God exhorts you to do! God is All-Hearing, All-Seeing. (Qur'an, 4:58)

Canon Taylor, one of the mission leaders of the Anglican Church, expresses the beauty revealed by the Islamic morality in one of his speeches as follows:

> It [Islam] brought out the fundamental dogmas of religion – the unity and greatness of God, that He is merciful and righteous, that He claims obedience to His will, resignation and faith. It proclaimed the responsibility of man, a future life, a day of judgment, and stern retribution to fall upon the wicked; and enforced the duties of prayer, almsgiving, fasting and benevolence. It thrust aside the artificial virtues, the religious frauds and follies, the perverted moral sentiments, and the verbal subtleties of theological disputants... It gave hope to the slave, brotherhood to mankind, and recognition to the fundamental facts of human nature.[9]

The false assertion that people in conquered countries converted to Islam under threat has also been disproved by Western researchers, and the justice

In the lands around Jerusalem, which have been under Muslim rule for long periods of time, peace and tolerance is now replaced by war and conflict.

and tolerant attitude of Muslims has been confirmed. L.Browne, a Western researcher, expresses this situation in the following words:

> Incidentally these well-established facts dispose of the idea so widely fostered in Christian writings that the Muslims, wherever they went, forced people to accept Islam at the point of the sword.[10]

In his book *The Prospects of Islam*, Browne goes on to say that the real motive behind the Muslims' conquests was the brotherhood of Islam. The vast majority of Muslim administrators who have reigned over the Muslim lands throughout history continued to treat the members of other religions with the utmost tolerance and respect. Within the borders of all Islamic states, both Jews and Christians lived in safety and enjoyed freedom.

Georgetown University's Professor of Religion and International Relations John L. Esposito describes how Jews and Christians who came under the administration of Muslim states met with enormous tolerance:

Muslim armies proved to be formidable conquerors and effective rulers, builders rather than destroyers. They replaced the indigenous rulers and armies of the conquered countries, but preserved much of their goverment, bureaucracy, and culture. For many in the conquered territories, it was no more than an exchange of masters, one that brought peace to peoples demoralized and disaffected by the casualties and heavy taxation that resulted from the years of Byzantine-Persian warfare. Local communities were free to continue to follow their own way of life in internal, domestic affairs. In many ways, local populations found Muslim rule more flexible and tolerant than that of Byzantium and Persia. Religious communities were free to practice their faith – to worship and be governed by their religious leaders and laws in such areas as marriage, divorce, and inheritance. In exchange, they were required to pay tribute, a poll tax (jizya) that entitled them to Muslim protection from outside aggression and exempted them from military service. They were therefore called the "protected ones" (dhimmmi). In effect, this often meant lower taxes, grater local autonomy, rule by fellow Semites with closer linguistic and cultural ties than the hellenized, Greco-Roman elites of Byzantium, and greater religious freedom for Jews and indigenous Christians. Most of the Christian churches, such as the Nestorians, Monophysites, Jacobites, and Copts, had been persecuted as heretics and schismatics by Christian orthodoxy. For these reasons, some Jewish and Christian communities aided the invading armies, regarding them as less oppressive than their imperial masters. In many ways, the conquests brought a Pax Islamica to an embattled area.[11]

Another "Pax Islamica" brought by Islam was to women, a segment of society that was tremendously abused in the pre-Islamic times. Professor Bernard Lewis, known to be one of the greatest Western experts on the Middle East, makes the following comment:

In general, the advent of Islam brought an enormous improvement in the position of women in ancient Arabia, endowing them with property and some other rights, and giving them a measure of protection against ill treatment by their husbands or owners. The killing of female infants, sanctioned by custom in Pagan Arabia, was outlawed by Islam. But the position of women remained poor, and worsened when, in this as in so many other respects, the original message of Islam lost its impetus and was modified under the influence of pre-existing attitudes and customs.[12]

The reign of the Seljuk Turks and that of the Ottoman Empire were also marked by the just and tolerant outlook of Islam. In his book, *The Spread of Islam in the World*, Sir Thomas Arnold, the British researcher, explains the Christians' willingness to come under Seljuk rule because of this attitude:

> This same sense of security of religious life under Muslim rule led many of the Christians of Asia Minor, also, about the same time, to welcome the advent of the Saljuq Turks as their deliverers… In the reign of Michael VIII (1261-1282), the Turks were often invited to take possession of the smaller towns in the interior of Asia Minor by the inhabitants, that they might escape from the tyranny of the empire; and both rich and poor often emigrated into Turkish dominions.[13]

Malik Shah, the ruler of the Islamic Seljuk Empire during its brightest age, approached the people in the conquered lands with great tolerance and compassion and thus was remembered with respect and love by them. All objective historians refer to the justice and tolerance of Malik Shah in their works. His tolerance also kindled feelings of love towards him in the hearts of the People of the Book. For this reason, unprecedented in history, many cities came under Malik Shah's rule of their own free will. Sir Thomas Arnold also mentions Odo de Diogilo, a monk of St. Denis, who participated in the Second

Many crusaders were surprised at the just, tolerant and compassionate attitude displayed by Muslims even on the battlefield. Later, they openly expressed their admiration in their memoirs. In the picture above we see the Second Crusade inaugurated by Louis VII.

Crusade as the private chaplain of Louis VII, refers in his memoirs to the justice administered by Muslims regardless of the subjects' religious affiliation. Based on the graphic account of Odo de Diogilo, Sir Thomas Arnold writes:

> The situation of the survivors would have been utterly hopeless, had not the sight of their misery melted the hearts of the Muhammadans to pity. They tended the sick and relieved the poor and starving with open-handed liberality. Some even bought up the French money which the Greeks had got out of the pilgrims by force or cunning, and lavishly distributed it among the needy. So great was the contrast between the kind treatment the pilgrims received from the unbelievers and the cruelty of their fellow-Christians, the Greeks, who imposed forced labour upon them, beat them, and robbed them of what little they had left, that many of them voluntarily embraced the faith of their deliverers. As the old chronicler [Odo de Diogilo] says: "Avoiding their co-religionists who had been so cruel to them, they went in safety among the infidels who had compassion upon them, and, as we heard, more than three thousand joined themselves to the Turks when they retired."[14]

These statements by historians reveal that Muslim administrators who truly adopted the morality of the Islam always ruled with tolerance, compassion and justice. Likewise, the history of the Ottoman Empire which ruled lands on three continents for centuries abounds with examples of tolerance.

The way the Jews settled in Ottoman lands during the time of Sultan Beyazid II, after being subjected to massacre and exile in the Catholic kingdoms of Spain and Portugal, is a fine example of the tolerance that Islamic morality brings with it. The Catholic monarchs who ruled much of Spain at the time brought grave pressure to bear on the Jews who had formerly lived in peace under Muslim rule in Andalusia. While Muslims, Christians and Jews were able to live side by side in peace in Andalusia, the Catholic monarchs tried to force the whole country to become Christian, and declared war on the Muslims while oppressing the Jews. As a result, the last Muslim ruler in the Granada region of southern Spain was overthrown in 1492. Muslims were subjected to terrible slaughter, and those Jews who refused to change their religion were sent into exile.

Muslim rule in Spain came to an end in 1492 when Granada was conquered by the armies of King Ferdinand and Queen Isabella. In the picture above, the surrender of the city is depicted.

One group of these Jews without a homeland sought shelter in the Ottoman Empire, and the state allowed them to do so. The Ottoman fleet, under the command of Kemal Reis, brought the exiled Jews, and those Muslims who had survived the slaughter, to the land of the Ottomans.

Sultan Beyazid II has gone down in history as a most pious believer, and in the spring of 1492 he settled these wronged Jews who had been expelled from Spain in certain parts of his empire, around Edirne, and Thessalonica in present-day Greece. Most of the 25,000 Turkish Jews living in Turkey today are the ancestors of those Spanish Jews. They have adapted their religion and customs, which they brought from Spain some 500 years ago, to the conditions in Turkey, and continue to live most comfortably with their own schools, hospitals, old people's homes, cultural associations and newspapers. In the same way that they have traders and businessmen, they also have representatives in numerous professions, from technical subjects to advertising, with increasingly developing intellectual circles. While Jewish

Sultan Beyazid II was a devout Muslim. He welcomed the Jews who were fleeing from Spanish persecution, and afforded them the freedom to practise their religion in Muslim lands.

communities in many countries in Europe have for centuries been exposed to the fear of anti-Semitic racist attacks, those in Turkey have lived in peace and security. This example alone is enough to demonstrate the tolerance that Islam brings with it and its understanding of justice.

The compassion and tolerance exhibited by Sultan Beyazid II applied to all the Ottoman sultans. When Sultan Mehmet the Conqueror captured Constantinople, he allowed the Christians and the Jews to live freely there. André Miquel, who is known for the valuable works he has written about the just and tolerant practices of Muslims and the world of Islam, says:

> The Christian communities lived under a well administered state that they did not have during the Byzantine and Latin periods. They were never subjected to systematic persecution. On the contrary, the empire and especially Istanbul had become a refuge for Spanish Jews who were tortured. People were never Islamized by force; the movements of Islamization took place as a result of social processes.[15]

As is clear from these facts, Muslims have at no time in history been oppressive. On the contrary, they have brought peace and security to all nations and beliefs wherever they have gone. They have abided by God's verse which says: **"Worship God and do not associate anything with Him. Be good**

The conquest of Istanbul by Sultan Mehmet the Conqueror meant freedom for Jews and heterodox Christians who had been subjected to oppression for centuries by Roman and Byzantine rulers.

to your parents and relatives and to orphans and the very poor, and <u>to neighbours who are related to you and neighbours who are not related to you</u>, and to companions and travellers and your slaves. God does not love anyone vain or boastful." (Qur'an, 4:36) and have behaved well to all people.

In short, friendship, brotherhood, peace and love are the bases of Qur'anic morality, and it is to these superior virtues that Muslims try to adhere. (For further details, see Harun Yahya's *Justice and Tolerance in the Qur'an*)

Sultan Mehmet the Conqueror granted many concessions to the Patriarchate. The Patriarch enjoyed autonomy for the first time in history, under Turkish rule. In the picture we see Sultan Mehmet the Conqueror receiving the Patriarch.

Those who believe and do not mix
up their belief with any wrongdoing,
they are the ones who are safe...
(Qur'an, 6:82)

THE REAL FACE OF THE TERRORISTS WHO ACT IN THE NAME OF RELIGION

All these examples reveal that organising acts of terror against innocent people is utterly against Islam and it is unlikely that any Muslim could ever commit such crime. On the contrary, Muslims are responsible for stopping these people, removing "mischief on earth" and bringing peace and security to all people all over the world.

It is not possible to talk about "Christian terror", "Jewish terror" or "Islamic terror". Indeed, an examination into the background of the perpetrators of these acts reveal that the terrorism in question is not a religious but a social phenomenon.

Crusaders: Barbarians Who Trampled Their Own Religion

The true message of a religion or a system of belief can be at times distorted by its own pseudo-adherents. The Crusaders, whose period constitutes a dark episode in Christian history, are an example of this type of distortion.

The Crusaders were European Christians who undertook expeditions from the end of the 11th century onwards to recover the Holy Land (Palestine and the surrounding area) from the Muslims. They set out with a so-called religious goal, yet they laid waste each acre of land they entered spreading fear wherever they went. They subjected civilians along their way to mass executions and plundered many villages and towns. Their conquest of Jerusalem, where Muslims, Jews and Christians lived under Islamic rule in peace, became the scene of immense bloodshed. They massacred all the Muslims and Jews in the city without mercy.

In the words of one historian, **"They killed all the Saracens and the Turks they found... whether male of female."**[16] One of the Crusaders, Raymond of Aguiles, boasted of this violence:

> Wonderful sights were to be seen. Some of our men (and this was more merciful) cut off the heads of their enemies; others shot them with arrows, so that they fell from the towers; others tortured them longer by casting them into the flames. **Piles of heads, hands and feet were to be seen in the streets of the city.** It was necessary to pick one's way over the bodies of men and horses. But these were small matters compared to what happened at the Temple of Solomon, a place where religious services are normally chanted ... in the Temple and porch of Solomon, **men rode in blood up to their knees and bridle reins.**[17]

In two days, the Crusader army killed some 40,000 Muslims in the barbaric ways just described.[18]

The Crusaders' barbarism was so excessive that, during the Fourth Crusade, they plundered Constantinople (present-day Istanbul), a Christian city, and stole the golden objects from the churches.

Of course, all this barbarism was utterly against Christian doctrine.

Under Muslim rule, Muslims, Jews and Orthodox Christians had lived together in peace in Jerusalem. When the Crusaders invaded Jerusalem (as seen above) they carried out terrible acts of slaughter. The Crusaders continued on to sack many more towns and murdering civilians as they went.

Christianity, in the words of the Bible, is a "message of love". In the Gospel according to Matthew, it is said that Jesus said to his followers, **"Love your enemies and pray for those who persecute you"** (Matthew, 5:44). In the Gospel according to Luke, it is said that Jesus said, **"To him who strikes you on the cheek, offer the other also."** (Luke, 6:29) In no part of the Gospels is there any reference to the legitimacy of violence; thus murdering innocent people is unimaginable. You can find

On September 12, 1204, the Crusaders entered Constantinople, which was held by their fellow Christians. They sacked and looted the city even to the extent of ripping the gold out of the churches.

the concept of "murdering the innocent" in the Bible; but only in the cruel Jewish King Herod's attempt to kill Jesus while he was a baby.

If Christianity is a religion based on love that accommodates no violence, how did Christian Crusaders carry out some of the most violent acts in history? The major reason for this was that the Crusaders were mainly made up of ignorant people who could better be defined as "rabble". These masses, who knew almost nothing about their religion, who had probably never read or even seen the Bible once in their lifetime, and who were for the most part completely unaware of the moral values of the Bible, were led into barbarism under the conditioning of Crusaders' slogans which presented this violence as "God's Will". Employing this fraudulent method, many were encouraged to commit dreadful acts strictly forbidden by the religion.

It is worth mentioning that in that period, Eastern Christians – the people of Byzantium, for instance – who were culturally far ahead of Western Christians, espoused more humane values. Both before and after the Crusaders' conquests, Orthodox Christians managed to live together with Muslims. According to Terry Jones, the BBC commentator, with the withdrawal of the Crusaders from Middle East, "civilized life started again and members of the three monotheistic faiths returned to peaceful coexistence."[19]

The example of the Crusaders is indicative of a general phenomenon. The more the adherents of an ideology are uncivilised, intellectually underdeveloped and ignorant, the more likely they are to resort to violence. This also holds true for ideologies that have nothing to do with religion. All communist movements around the world are prone to violence. Yet the most savage and bloodthirsty of them were the Red Khmers in Cambodia. This was because they were the most ignorant.

The Bedouin Character in the Qur'an

In the period of the Prophet Muhammad, there existed two basic social structures in Arabia. City-dwellers and Bedouins (desert Arabs). A sophisticated culture prevailed in Arab towns. Commercial relations linked the towns to the outer world, which contributed to the formation of "good manners" among Arabs dwelling in cities. They had refined aesthetic values, enjoyed literature and especially poetry. Desert Arabs, on the other hand, were the nomad tribes living in the desert who had a very crude culture. Utterly unaware of arts and literature, they developed an unrefined character.

Islam was born and developed among the inhabitants of Mecca, the most important city of the peninsula. However, as Islam spread to the rest of the the peninsula, all the tribes in Arabia embraced it. Among these tribes were also desert Arabs, who were somehow problematic: their poor intellectual and cultural background prevented some of them from grasping the profundity and noble spirit of Islam. Of this God states the following in a verse:

> **The desert Arabs are the worst in disbelief and hypocrisy, and more fitted to be ignorant of the limits which God has sent down to His Messenger. But God is Knowing, Wise. (Qur'an, 9:97)**

The desert Arabs, that is, social groups who were "worst in disbelief and hypocrisy" and prone to disobey God's commands, became a part of the Islamic world in the Prophet's time. However, in later periods, they became a source of trouble for the house of Islam. The sect called "Kharijis" that emerged among the Bedouins was an example. The most distinctive trait of this perverse sect (which was called "Kharijis", the "rebels", because they greatly

Bedouins were nomadic tribes of the desert at the time of the Prophet Muhammad. Because of the harsh conditions in which they lived, they came to possess a hard and rough culture.

deviated from Sunni practices), was their wild and fanatical nature. The "Kharijis", who had little understanding of the essence of Islam or of the virtues and the values of the Qur'an, waged war against all other Muslims basing this war on a few Qur'anic verses about which they made distorted interpretations. Furthermore, they carried out "acts of terrorism". Ali, who was one of the closest companions of the Prophet and was described as the "gate of the city of knowledge", was assassinated by a Kharijite.

In later periods, "Hashashis", another brutal organisation, emerged; this was a "terrorist organisation" made up of ignorant and fanatical militants bereft of a profound understanding of the essence of Islam and thus who could be readily influenced by simple slogans and promises.

In other words, just as the Crusaders distorted and misinterpreted Christianity as a teaching of brutality, some perverted groups emerging in the Islamic world misinterpreted Islam and resorted to brutality. What is common to these sects and the Crusaders was their "Bedouin" nature. That is, they were ignorant, unrefined and uncultivated, lacking a true understanding of their religion. The violence they resorted to resulted from this lack of understanding, rather than from the religion they claimed to espouse.

A Terrorist is Without Pity Whose Only Purpose is to Destroy

The founder of Russian Anarchy, Michael Bakunin and his disciple Nechayev define an ideal terrorist in this way:

The whole work of his [a revolutionist's] existence, not only in words, but also in deeds, is at war with the existing order of society, and with the whole so-called civilized world, with its laws, morals and customs, he is an uncompromising opponent... He knows only one science; the science of destruction. (The Alarm Newspaper Article, "Bakunin's Ground-Work for the Social Revolution," 1885 Dec. 26, p. 8)

As understood from these words of Bakunin and Nechayev, terrorists are people who sever their relationship with every material and spiritual institution thereby rejecting every moral value, and who view these institutions as impediments to their designs. Bakunin also said, **"Day and night dare he [a revolutionist] have only one thought, one aim: the unmerciful destruction; while he, cold-blooded and without rest, follows that aim, he himself must be ready to die at any time and ready to kill with his own hands any one who seeks to thwart his aims."** In his *Ground-Work for the Social Revolution*, there is this description of what kind of person a terrorist must be:

Stringent with himself he must also be to others. All weak sentiment towards relation, friendship, love and thankfulness must be suppressed through the only cold passion of the revolutionary work.

These words lay bare the dark face of terrorism and show that it is completely opposed to the religion of Islam which is founded on peace, tolerance and love. In this verse, God reveals that peace is the real salvation of humanity and that pursuing the opposite, that is war and conflict, is to walk in the steps of Satan:

O You who believe! Enter absolutely into peace (Islam). Do not follow in the footsteps of Satan. He is an outright enemy to you. (Qur'an, 2:208)

Michael Bakunin

The Mass Psychology of Terrorism

Another important characteristic of terrorists is that they act with a collective spirit. Within this spirit, individual ideas and personal choice are disregarded as everyone is directed toward one single goal. Those who act within this collective spirit may do things they would never do in their right mind and commit acts without using their own will and consciousness. In many countries of the world, terror groups composed of a few unintelligent and uneducated people get caught up in the emotional hysteria of mass meetings, slogans, and without even knowing what they are doing or why, they get involved in committing mass atrocities. In one moment, such people can turn into killers with blood on their hands, and even terrorists who are able to commit inhumane acts. A person may seem quiet and calm when he is alone, but when he becomes a part of a terrorist group, he may become capable of committing acts of arson and assault for no apparent reason. Such spells are cast over individuals that they are even willing to be killed for their cause. The majority of those who take part in acts of terror often have weak wills and consciences, and they become like a flock of sheep under the influence of mass psychology. Good sense and judgment are substituted by excessive and extravagant emotionalism and a tendency toward violence and aggression. Such people are easily provoked, intolerant and know no limitation set by any law.

The error of this mass psychology is revealed in the Qur'an where it says that human beings must act according to their own will and intelligence:

Do not pursue what you have no knowledge of. Hearing, sight and hearts will all be questioned. (Qur'an, 17:36)

One of the Sources of Terrorism: Third World Fanaticism

These examples from history may help us gain better understanding of the present phenomenon, the so-called "Islamic terror", which is nowadays at the top of the international agenda. That is because those who emerge and carry out acts of terrorism in the name of Islam and those who back such acts, representing a tiny minority in the world of Islam, stem from this "character peculiar to Bedouins", not from Islam itself. Failing to understand the essence of Islam, which is essentially a religion of peace and justice, they make it a tool of barbarism, which is simply an outcome of their social and cultural structure. The origin of this barbarism, which may well be called "Third World Fanaticism", is the benighted initiatives of people who are devoid of love for their fellow human-beings.

It is a fact that, for the last few centuries, Muslims in all corners of the Islamic world, have been subjected to violence by Western forces and their allies. The colonialist European states, local oppressive regimes or colonialists backed by the West (Israel, for example) have caused great suffering to Muslims at large. However, for Muslims, this is a situation that has to be approached and responded to from a purely Qur'anic stance.

In no part of the Qur'an does God command believers to respond to violence with violence. On the contrary, God commands Muslims to "respond to evil with goodness":

A good deed and a bad deed are not the same. Repel the bad with something better and, if there is enmity between you and someone else, he will be like a bosom friend. (Qur'an, 41:34)

It is no doubt a legitimate right of Muslims to react against this cruelty. However, these reactions should never turn into a blind hatred, an unjust enmity. God warns about this in the following verse:

... Let not the hatred of a people [who once] obstructed you from the Sacred Mosque lead you to transgress. Help one another in benevolence and piety, and help not one another in sin and transgression... (Qur'an, 5:2)

Consequently, carrying out terrorist acts against the innocent people of other nations under the pretence of "representing the innocent nations in the world", is by no means compatible with Islam.

Another point that deserves a special mention here is that all Western nations and communities cannot be held responsible for the aforementioned violence and oppression against Muslims. Actually, the materialist, irreligious philosophies and ideologies that prevailed in the 19th century are in the main responsible for these dismal acts. European colonialism did not originate from Christianity. On the contrary, anti-religious movements opposing the values of Christianity led the way to colonialism. At the roots of the greatest brutalities of the 19th century lies the Social Darwinist ideology. In the Western world today, there are still cruel, mischievous and opposing factors, as well as a culture dominated by peaceful and just elements that have its roots in Christianity. As a matter of fact, the main disagreement is not between the West and Islam. Contrary to the general opinion, it is between the devout people of the West and of the Muslim world on the one hand, and the people opposing religion (materialists, atheists, Darwinists etc.) on the other.

Another indication that Third World Fanaticism has nothing to do with Islam is that, until recently, this fanaticism had been identified with the communist ideology. As is well-known, similar anti-Western acts of terror were carried out in 1960s and 1970s by Soviet-backed communist organisations. As the impact of the communist ideology faded, some of the social structures which gave birth to communist organisations have turned their attention to Islam. This "brutality presented under the guise of religion", which is formulated by the incorporation of some Islamic concepts and symbols into the former communist literature is entirely against the moral values which constitute the essence of Islam.

A last remark about this issue is that Islam is not peculiar to a particular nation or geographical region. Contrary to the dominant Western perception, Islam is not an "eastern culture". Islam is the last religion revealed to mankind as a guide to the true path that recommends itself to all humanity. Muslims are responsible for communicating the true religion they believe in to all people of all nations and cultures and making them feel closer to Islam.

Consequently, there is a unique solution for people and groups who, in the name of Islam, resort to terror, form oppressive regimes and turn this world into a dreadful place instead of beautifying it: revealing the true nature of Islam and communicating it so that the masses can understand and live by it.

One of The Methods of Terrorism is to Cause Fear and Panic in Society

One of the most important characteristics of terrorism is that it selects its targets indiscriminately. The fact that it determines these targets without discrimination is one of the most important reasons for the spread of fear, because no one can feel secure. If people know that they are possible targets for no reasons, no one will feel safe from the terrorists. There is nothing a potential target can do to protect themselves, since terrorists act according to their own rules, in a time and place of their own choosing. Thus acts of terror in society are arbitrary and unpredictable.

Terrorist organisations attack their targets indiscriminately which means that innocent and defenceless individuals are killed or wounded. A typical example of this was the nerve gas attack in the Tokyo Metro on March 20, 1995.

The Error of Radicalism

There is another idea that we must examine together with that of terror; that is, the phenomenon of radicalism.

Radicalism means supporting sudden revolutionary destructive changes in any sphere and applying a strict uncompromising policy in order to achieve them. Radicals are characterised by their desire for revolutionary change and the stern, sometimes aggressive attitude they adopt.

In this, as in every sphere of life, the guide for the Muslim is the Qur'an. When we look at radicalism in the light of the Qur'an, we see that it has nothing to do with the way in which God commands the believers to behave. When God describes a believer in the Qur'an, He depicts him as a loving, soft-spoken person, shunning conflicts and arguments, approaching even the most hostile people with warmth and friendship.

An example to guide us in this matter is the command given by God to Moses and Aaron to go to Pharaoh and speak gently to him:

Go to Pharaoh; he has overstepped the bounds. But speak to him with gentle words so that hopefully he will pay heed or show some fear. (Qur'an, 20:43-44)

Pharaoh was one of the most cruel and rebellious unbelievers of his time. He was a despot who denied God and worshipped idols; moreover, he subjected believers (the Israelites of the time) to terrible cruelties and murder. But God commanded His prophets to go to such a hostile man and speak to him gently.

You will notice that the way shown by God was the way of friendly dialogue, not the way of conflict with sharp words, angry slogans and agitated protests.

There are a few other examples to show Muslims how to behave in the dialogue between Shu'ayb and the deniers. This dialogue is related in the Qur'an in this way:

And to Madyan their brother Shu'ayb. He said, "My people, worship God! You have no deity apart from Him. Do not give short measure and short weight. I see you prospering and I fear for you the punishment of an all-encompassing Day.

God
commands you to return to
their owners the things you hold in
trust and, when you judge between people,
to judge with justice. How excellent is what
God exhorts you to do! God is All-
Hearing, All-Seeing.
(Qur'an, 4:58)

My people! Give full measure and full weight with justice; do not diminish people's goods; and do not go about the earth, corrupting it.

What endures with God is better for you if you are believers. I am not set over you as your keeper."

They said, "Shu'ayb, do your prayers instruct you that we should abandon what our fathers worshipped or stop doing whatever we want to with our wealth? Yet you are such a lenient, normal person!"

He said, "My people! What do you think? If I do possess a Clear Sign from my Lord and He has given me His good provision, I do not want to oppose you in what way I am forbidding you. I only want to put things right as far as I can. My success is with God alone. I have put my trust in Him and I turn to Him." (Qur'an, 11:84-88)

When we examine what he says, we see that Shu'ayb invited the people to believe in God and to adopt high moral principals and he did this with friendliness and humility. We can explain some of the reasons behind of the things said in these verses:

* When Shu'ayb says **"I am not set over you as your keeper**." to the people, he does not want to dominate them; his only intention is to inform them of the truth that God has revealed.

* **"You are clearly the forbearing, the rightly-guided"**: These words of the deniers to Shu'ayb show his warm, gentle and courteous character and that this was particularly appreciated by the deniers.

* **"My people! What do you think?"** This expression used by Shu'ayb shows that he calls on the deniers to use their intelligence and conscience. In other words, he does not use insistent pressure, but questions their ideas from an opposing stance and invites them to consider and come to a conclusion based on their own free conscience.

* **"I do not want to oppose you in what way I am forbidding you"**. Shu'ayb's prohibition here is not actually a prohibition. He explains that some acts are sinful and invites the people to abandon them. Moreover, when Shu'ayb says **"I do not want to oppose you"**, it is not his purpose to dispute with the people; he does not want to make them uncomfortable and incite a quarrel; he wants only to invite them to faith and the practice of high moral principles.

If you examine the Qur'an you will see that a warm, gentle and tolerant disposition characterized all the prophets. God describes Abraham as **"tender-hearted and forbearing."** (Qur'an, 9:114) and in another verse, the prophet Muhammad's moral principles are described in this way:

> **It is a mercy from God that you were gentle with them. If you had been rough or hard of heart, they would have scattered from around you. So pardon them and ask forgiveness for them, and consult with them about the matter. Then when you have reached a firm decision, put your trust in God. God loves those who put their trust in Him. (Qur'an, 3:159)**

An obvious characteristic of radicalism is its anger. This disposition can be clearly seen in the speeches, writings and demonstrations of radicals. However, anger is not an attribute of Muslims. When God describes believers in the Qur'an, he describes, **"those who give in times of both ease and hardship, those who control their rage and pardon other people – God loves the good-doers"** (Qur'an, 3:134)

There is no situation in which a Muslim displays anger. The only thing a Muslim wants from other people is that they believe in God and live according to moral principles, but this is possible only by the grace of God. No matter what we do, no matter how much we try to explain the truth to people, human hearts are in God's hands. God reminds Muslims of this very important fact in this verse, **"... Do those who believe not know that if God had wanted to He could have guided all mankind? ..."** (Qur'an, 13:31)

There is another verse that emphasises this same fact;

> **If your Lord had willed, all the people on the earth would have believed. Do you think you can force people to be believers? (Qur'an, 10:99)**

Therefore, it is the duty of a Muslim only to explain the facts and to invite people to accept them. Whether or not people accept the invitation is completely up to their own conscience. God reveals this truth in the Qur'an when He says that there is no compulsion in religion.

> **There is no compulsion in religion. True guidance has become clearly distinct from error. Anyone who rejects false deities and has belief in God has grasped the Firmest Handhold, which will never give way. God is All-Hearing, All-Knowing. (Qur'an, 2:256)**

For terrorists, killing people, wreaking destruction and havoc is a way of life. For them, bloodshed is a deliberate act. They can shoot innocents, throw a bomb at children or blow up a house without any feeling of compassion.

Therefore, there is no coercion to make people believe and become Muslims, or to make Muslims perform prayers and beware of sin. There is only advice. God reveals in a few verses addressed to the Messenger of God that Muslims are not oppressors:

> We know best what they say. You are not a dictator over them. So remind, with the Qur'an, whoever fears My Threat. (Qur'an, 50:45)

> Say: "Mankind! The truth has come to you from your Lord. Whoever is guided is only guided for his own good. Whoever is misguided is only misguided to his detriment. I have not been set over you as a guardian." (Qur'an, 10:108)

Muslims are responsible only for explaining their religion, they apply no pressure or coercion on anyone and are enjoined to speak gently to even the most tyrannical deniers. Such persons cannot be radicals, because radicalism stands for the opposite of those qualities we have enumerated. Indeed, radicalism is an unIslamic current of thought and a political stance that came into the Islamic world from outside. When we examine social phenomena described in terms of radicalism, it will be seen that these are **basically a collection of methods and pronouncements used by communists in the past**, or an expression of the **"fanatical rage"** that has no place in true Islam. (The Qur'an, 48:26)

All Muslims must totally reject an angry, unbending argumentative attitude which goes against the very nature of the Qur'an and in its place adopt a friendly, gentle, tolerant, calm and compassionate one. Muslims must set an example to the world and be admired for their maturity, tolerance, moderation, modesty and peacefulness. Muslims must live Islam in the best possible way and be its representatives to the world, not only in these things, but also by their achievements in the fields of science, culture, art, aesthetics and social order and others.

Explaining Islam to others and defending Islam against ideas alien to it are included in what we have listed above. In the verse below, God clearly reveals what attitude a Muslim must assume with regard to others:

Call to the way of your Lord with wisdom and fair admonition, and argue with them in the kindest way. Your Lord knows best who is misguided from His way. And He knows best who are guided. (Qur'an, 16:125)

Terrorist Methods and Psychology

The concept of terror has a wider meaning in today's language. Generally it refers to the armed conflict carried on by radical ideological groups. In general, terror means intimidation. But this intimidation encompasses a broad field including the whole lives of people who feel the intense threat of fear and violence. Terror includes intense and systematic intimidation designed to make people adopt a certain way of thinking and behaviour, as well as every kind of violent act carried out to produce this intimidation. But in every situation, the target of terrorism is directly or indirectly the citizens themselves.

Terror organisations use terror to rally support. The intimidation they use is calculated to increase their strength and so to gain the support of some or all the citizens.

The first thing that people think of when we mention the word "terror" is generally the kind known as "leftist terror", but there is also a kind of terror found in Third World countries and practiced by dictatorial regimes. Actually the reality here is nothing other than a massive implementation of leftist terror tactics. A dictator or a group in power is oppressive, using their power only for personal gain and for this reason they experience various kinds of social opposition. In this situation, the dictatorial regime always resorts to the same formula to show that it is stronger than the opposition; they inaugurate the use of terror so that citizens will be afraid and their own power are consolidated.

Terror organisations, on the other hand, in accordance with the ideologies they espouse, claim that their aim is to remove a government and its administrators which they regard as illegitimate and cruel and, in so doing, that they will reach their goal of establishing a happier and more just way of life. However, this is not a realistic claim. In the Qur'an, in the first verses of Sura Baqara, God issues this command to those who think in this way:

When they are told, "Do not cause corruption on the earth," they say, "We are only putting things right." No indeed! They are the corrupters, but they are not aware of it. (Qur'an, 2:11-12)

For terrorists, killing people is a way of life. They may shoot innocent people without pity and throw bombs at children. For them shedding blood is a pleasure. They have ceased to be human beings and turned into raving savage beasts. If there is anyone among them who shows the least feeling of compassion, they brand him as a coward or a traitor and demote him. Often they use their guns against one another and carry out bloody purges against internal factions in their own organisation.

It can be seen that terrorism is nothing other than a totally diabolical source of bloodshed. Whoever supports this cycle of savagery is defending a

Terrorists aim to damage people both physically and psychologically to attain a certain goal. Morals of religion, however, is opposed to terrorism in that it aims to foster love, well-being, compassion, joy and hope in society.

In the moral teaching of the Qur'an, to kill an innocent person is an act of immense cruelty. God forbids terrorist acts and condemns those who commit them.

satanic system. If a terrorist uses religious language and symbols, this must not deceive anyone. Terrorists who hide under the cloak of false religion are doubly guilty, both of the blood they have shed and for the anti-religious propaganda they have spread while committing these crimes in the name of religion.

Terror and religion are completely opposed to each other. Terrorism adopts the way of aggression, murder, conflict, cruelty and misery. But according to the Qur'an, all these things are kinds of oppression. God enjoins peace, harmony, goodwill and compromise. He forbids terror and every kind of act that does not promote peace, and, condemns those who commit such acts:

> **But as for those who break God's contract after it has been agreed and sever what God has commanded to be joined, and cause corruption in the earth, the curse will be upon them. They will have the Evil Abode. (Qur'an, 13:25)**

The basic quality that terror and those who are infected by its cruelty have in common is that the fear and love of God is something completely alien to them. Their hearts have become hardened and they are spiritually ill. In the Qur'an, God speaks about the character of such people:

> **But do not obey any vile swearer of oaths, any backbiter, slandermonger, impeder of good, evil aggressor, gross, coarse and furthermore, despicable.(Qur'an, 68:10-13)**

To rebel for no cause and to commit acts of assault are forbidden by God. In Islam, acts of what we call terror and anarchy today are forbidden. In the Qur'an it is said:

> **Say: "My Lord has forbidden indecency, both open and hidden, and wrong action, and unrightful tyranny, and associating anything with God for which He has sent down no authority, and saying things about God that you do not know." (Qur'an, 7:33)**

...Heed God (alone). God is
aware of what you do.

(Qur'an, 5:8)

Acts of Violence-
One of the Most
Important Methods of
Terrorist Propoganda

Terrorists regard acts of violence as propaganda for their organisations. For them, killing innocent people, robbing banks, assassinating people, kidnapping and planting bombs all act as propaganda for their struggle. To the terrorist who is bent on wreaking chaos, what publicity a single act of violence can generate in one day is much more publicity than what millions of brochures could do.

This idea is totally foreign to every kind of human feeling of compassion, mercy, concord and tolerance; it is alien to the moral teaching of the Qur'an and can gain a following only in those societies in which anti-religious ideologies hold sway. For this reason, the only possible solution that can save humanity from this benighted way of thinking is the widespread acceptance of the moral teachings found in the Qur'an and taken as a way of life.

Terrorists see their destructive acts as a means of propaganda; they hope to spread fear by destroying people and property.

God calls to the Abode of Peace and He guides whom He wills to a straight path. (Qur'an, 10:25)

THE OUTLOOK OF ISLAM ON THE PEOPLE OF THE BOOK

Another important topic that has been on the agenda with the acts of terrorism against the United States is the relation between the Western and Islamic worlds. As is known, by the 90s, some intellectuals were suggesting that the world was due for a struggle that would take place between the West and Islam. This is the basic theme of Samuel Huntington's well-known thesis "The Clash of Civilisations". However, this thesis – better called as "Clash of Ignorance" by Edward W. Said – rests on an imaginary scenario generated by the exaggeration of the influence of some radical and ignorant factions to be found in these two civilisations. Actually, there can be no clash between the Western civilisation and the Islamic civilisation, because the beliefs of Judaism and Christianity, the tenets upon which Western civilisation is based, are in perfect harmony with Islam.

In the Qur'an, Jews and Christians are called the "People of the Book". This is because the members of these two religions abide by the Divine Books revealed by God. The outlook of Islam on the People of the Book is extremely just and compassionate.

This attitude towards the People of the Book developed during the years of the birth of Islam. At that time, Muslims were a minority, struggling to protect their faith and suffering oppression and torture from the pagans of the city of Mecca. Due to this persecution, some Muslims decided to flee Mecca and shelter in a safe country with a just ruler. The Prophet Muhammad told them to take refuge the Christian king of Ethiopia. The Muslims who went to Ethiopia found a very fair administration that embraced them with love and respect. The King refused the demands of the pagan messengers who had travelled to Ethiopia and asked him to surrender the Muslims to them, and announced that Muslims could live freely in his country.

These Christian attitudes of compassion, mercy, and justice, are referred to in a verse of the Qur'an which states:

… You will find the people most affectionate to those who believe are those who say, "We are Christians." That is because some of them are priests and monks and because they are not arrogant. (Qur'an, 5:82)

Common Beliefs and Values Shared by Muslims and the People of the Book

Christian and Muslim beliefs have many aspects in common. Judaism too shares many beliefs with Islam. In the Qur'an, God relates that Muslims share the same faith with the People of the Book and that they say to them **"We have faith in what has been sent down to us and what was sent down to you. Our God and your God are one and we submit to Him."** (Qur'an, 29:46)

All true adherents of these three great religions:

✱ believe that God has created the entire universe out of nothing and that He dominates all that exists with His omnipotence.

✱ believe that God has created man and living things in a miraculous way and that man possesses a soul granted him by God.

In the Qur'an, Christians and Jews are defined as the People of the Book, and there is a command to show respect, mercy and kindness to them. Both Christians and Jews believe in God and share the same moral values as Muslims.

* believe in resurrection, Heaven and Hell and angels, and that God has created our lives with a certain destiny.

* believe that besides Jesus, Moses or Muhammad, God sent many prophets such as Noah, Abraham, Isaac and Joseph throughout history, and they love all these prophets.

In one verse, that Muslims make no distinction among prophets is related as follows:

> The Messenger believes in what has been sent down to him by his Lord, and so do the believers. Each one believes in God and His angels and His Books and His Messengers. We do not differentiate between any of His Messengers. They say, "We hear and we obey. Forgive us, our Lord! You are our journey's end." (Qur'an, 2:285)

The beliefs of the People of the Book are in harmony with Muslims, not only in terms of faith-related issues, but also of moral values. Today, in a world where such immoralities as adultery, homosexuality, drug addiction and a model of egoism and self-seeking cruelty have grown widespread, the People of the Book and Muslims share the same virtues: Honour, chastity, humility, self-sacrifice, honesty, compassion, mercy and unconditional love.

The Common Forces against Faith

Another important fact that draws Christianity, Judaism and Islam together is the atheist philosophies that are so influential in our time.

Among the best-known and most harmful philosophies of our age can be

Today both the Muslims and the People of the Book are engaged in a broadening struggle against immoralities such as sexual perversions or drug addiction. Each of these three religions accepts chastity, honesty and self-sacrifice as the greatest virtues.

cited materialism, communism, fascism, anarchism, racism, nihilism and existentialism. Many people who believed in the false diagnoses, deceptive descriptions and explanations of these ideas on the universe, society and man, have lost their faith or doubted it. What is more, these ideologies have dragged people, societies and nations into great crises, conflicts and wars. Their share of the blame for the pain and troubles that humanity suffers from today is immense.

While they deny God and creation, all the above-mentioned ideologies are based on a common framework, a so-called scientific basis; Charles Darwin's theory of evolution. Darwinism constitutes the basis of atheist philosophies. This theory claims that living beings have evolved as a result of coincidences and by means of a struggle for life. Therefore, Darwinism sends this deceptive message to people:

"You are not responsible to anyone, you owe your life to coincidences, you need to struggle, and if necessary to oppress others to succeed. This world is one of conflict and self-interest".

The social messages put across by Darwinist concepts such as "Natural selection", "struggle for life", "survival of the fittest" are a means of indoctrination. This evil morality advises people to be egoistical, self-seeking, cruel and oppressive. It destroys such virtues as mercy, compassion, self-sacrifice and humility, the moral values of the three great monotheistic religions and presents this as a necessity of "the rules of life."

This Darwinist indoctrination is just the opposite of the beliefs of the People of the Book and the message of the Qur'an. Consequently, the Darwinist indoctrination constitutes the foundation of a world which inherently opposes all the three divine religions.

This being the case, it is necessary for the People of the Book and Muslims to co-operate, since they believe in God and accept the morality that He teaches. The followers of these three religions should expose to the world the fallacy of Darwinism, which has no scientific basis, but which people are trying to preserve for the sake of materialist philosophy. They should co-operatively carry out an intellectual struggle against all other deceptive ideas (communism, fascism, racism) that serve atheism. Once this is realized, the world will, in a very short time, embrace peace, tranquillity and justice.

Godless ideologies such as fascism, communism, racism and anarchism have brought destruction upon humanity and have encouraged hatred within societies.

Darwinism proposes a society in which conflict and violence are seen as means of development. But a study of its effects on society reveals that the Social Darwinist project has only brought pain and destruction.

Antisemitism is a Racism Totally Contrary to Islam

In our times, antisemitism is an ideology which threatens world peace and targets the well-being and security of innocent people. This is racist hatred felt by some for the Jews.

In the 20th century, antisemitism signed its name to great disasters, one of the most horrible being the cruelty and murder inflicted on the Jews by the Nazis. In addition to this, in many countries authoritarian regimes have targeted Jews and subjected them to cruel treatment. Fascist organisations have harassed Jews and carried out bloody attacks against them.

So how should a Muslim regard antisemitism?

The persecution of Jews throughout history was basically a consequence of racist prejudices, which are definitely contrary to Islam. It is right to oppose and criticize the brutality of Israel, but no Muslim should condone unjust or cruel treatment of innocent Jewish people.

The answer is obvious. **Every Muslim must oppose antisemitism as he would oppose every other racist ideology.** Although Muslims justly condemn the cruel and aggressive policies of the State of Israel together with their occupation of adjacent territory, to blanket condemn innocent Jews is not acceptable to Muslims: this would be a symptom of antisemitism. However, criticising official Zionist ideology has nothing to do with antisemitism, since to object to Zionism is to object to an intense form of racism. There are many Jews who also criticise the racist policies of Zionism, and to label them as being antisemetic would be absurd.

Never subjecting a community to a blanket criticism is a command stressed in the Qur'an, there is a need to distinguish between the righteous and the wicked, the cruel ones and the innocent. After referring to some Jews and Christians, who violated God's commands, God also mentions some other Jews and Christians who displayed moral perfection:

> **[However] They are not all alike. Among the People of the Book there is an upright community who recite the revelation of God during the night and fall prostrate before Him. They believe in God and the Last Day, enjoin what is right and forbid what is evil, and vie with one another in good works. They are of the righteous. And whatever good they do, its reward will not be denied them. God knows those who fear [Him]. (Qur'an, 3:113-115)**

Antisemitism is an anti-religion ideology that has its roots in neo-paganism. Therefore, it is unthinkable that a Muslim would espouse antisemitism or feel sympathy for this ideology. Anti-Semites have no respect for Abraham, Moses or David who were blessed prophets chosen by God to be examples for humanity.

Antisemitism and other kinds of racism (eg. prejudice against blacks) have no place in true religion; they are perversions arising from various ideologies and superstitions.

Furthermore, when we examine antisemitism and other forms of racism, we see clearly that they promote ideas and a model of society that is totally contrary to the moral teachings of the Qur'an, for example, at the root of antisemitism lie hatred, violence, and lack of compassion. An anti-Semite may be so cruel as to support the murder of Jewish people, men, women, children and the aged, and condone their being subjected to torture. However, the moral teaching of the Qur'an enjoins love, compassion and mercy for all people. It also commands Muslims to show justice and be forgiving even to their enemies.

On the other hand, anti-Semites and other kinds of racists bulk at living together in peace with people of a different race or creed. (eg. German racists (Nazis) and Jewish racists (Zionists) were opposed to Germans and Jews living together; each side rejected this in the name of their respective race as a degeneration.) However, in the Qur'an, there is not the slightest distinction between races; the Qur'an advises that people of different faiths live together in the same society in peace and happiness.

Muslims want Jews, Christians and themselves to live in peace and contentment, treating each other with tolerance, friendship, respect and compassion.

According to the Qur'an, Muslims, Jews and Christians Must Live in Friendship

In the Qur'an, there is a significant difference between the People of the Book and those who have no belief in God. This is especially emphasised in the area of social life. For example, it is said concerning those who associate others with God: **"(they) are unclean, so after this year they should not come near the Sacred Mosque."** (Qur'an, 9:28) Those who associate others with God are people who know no divine law, have no moral precepts and who can commit every kind of degrading and perverse deed without hesitation.

But the People of the Book, while they rely basically on God's revelation, have moral precepts and know what is lawful and what is not. In the same way, permission has been given to a Muslim man to marry a woman from among the People of the Book. On this subject God commands:

> **Today all good things have been made lawful for you. And the food of those given the Book is also lawful for you and your food is lawful for them. So are chaste women from among the believers and chaste women of those given the Book before you, once you have given them their dowries in marriage, not in fornication or taking them as lovers. But as for anyone who disbelieves, his actions will come to nothing and in the hereafter he will be among the losers. (Qur'an, 5:5)**

These commands show that bonds of kinship may be established as a result of the marriage of a Muslim with a woman from the People of the Book and that those on each side of the union can accept an invitation to a meal. These are the fundamentals that will ensure **the establishment of equitable human relationships and a happy communal life.** Since the Qur'an enjoins this equitable and tolerant attitude, it is unthinkable that a Muslim could take an opposing view.

The just and tolerant practices of the Prophet Muhammad towards the people of the Book set very good examples to Muslims. In the contract made with the Christians of Najran, who lived in the south of Arabia, the Prophet Muhammad demonstrates one of the best examples of tolerance and justice. The contract included the following article:

> The lives of the people of Najran and its surrounding area, their religion, their land, property, cattle and those of them who are present or absent, their messengers and their places of worship are under the protection of Allah and guardianship of His Prophet.[20]

By means of such contracts, the Messenger of God secured a social order for Muslims and the People of the Book alike, which was marked by peace and security. This order was a total manifestation of the following verse:

> **Those who believe, those who are Jews, and the Christians and Sabaeans, all who believe in God and the Last Day and act rightly, will have their reward with their Lord. They will feel no fear and will know no sorrow. (Qur'an, 2:62)**

The Constitution of Madinah is the most important contract that secured justice and tolerance among Christians, Jews and pagan communities.

The Constitution of Madinah was prepared under the leadership of the Prophet Muhammad 1,400 years ago, that is in 622 AD, to meet the needs of people of different beliefs, and was put into practice as a written legal contract. Different communities of different religions and races that had harboured deep-seated enmity towards one another for 120 years became parties to this legal contract. By means of this contract, the Prophet Muhammad showed that conflicts between those societies, who had been enemies and quite unable to reach any form of compromise, could come to an end, and they could actually live side by side.

At the time of the Prophet Muhammad, a just and tolerant policy was practised in relation to the People of the Book.

According to the Constitution of Madinah, everyone was free to adhere to any belief or religion or to make any political or philosophical choice. People sharing the same views could come together and form a community. Everyone was free to exercise his own justice system. However, anyone who committed a crime would be protected by no one. The parties to the contract would engage in co-operation with one another, provide support for each other, and would remain under the protection of the Prophet Muhammad. Conflicts between the parties would be brought to the Messenger of God.

This contract was in force from 622 to 632 AD. Through this document, the tribal structures which had formerly been based on blood and kinship were abolished, and people of different cultural, ethnical and geographical backgrounds came together and formed a social unity. The Constitution of Madinah secured absolute religious freedom.

Monasteries, Churches and Synagogues Must Be Respected

Another important fact we learn from the Qur'an is that Muslims must respect Jewish and Christian places of worship. In the Qur'an, the places of worship of the People of the Book, ie. monasteries, churches and synagogues, are mentioned as places of worship protected by God.

...if God had not driven some people back by means of others, monasteries, churches, synagogues and mosques, where God's name is mentioned much, would have been pulled down and destroyed. God will certainly help those who help Him – God is All-Strong, Almighty. (Qur'an, 22:40)

This verse shows every Muslim the importance of respecting and protecting the holy places of the People of the Book.

Indeed, the Prophet Muhammad also made contracts with pagans as well as the people of the Book. Pagans were always treated with justice, and when they asked to be taken under protection, their requests were readily accepted by Muhammad. This meant that these communities sought the protection of the Messenger of God in the face of an attack or a wrongful accusation. Throughout his life, many non-Muslims and pagans requested protection from the Prophet Muhammad, and he took them under his protection and ensured their security. In Sura Tawba, God advises that requests of pagans seeking protection be accepted by believers. Of this, God says the following:

If any of the idolaters ask you for protection, give them protection until they have heard the words of God. Then convey them to a place where they are safe... (Qur'an, 9:6)

Jews and Christians, due to their shared commonalities with Muslims are much closer to Muslims than those who have no faith in God. Each of these religions has its book, that is, they are subject to a book sent down by God. They know what is right and what is wrong, what is lawful and what is unlawful according to their scriptures, and all revere the Prophets and Messengers that accompanied them. They all believe in a hereafter, and afterlife where they will have to give an account to God for all their actions. So, there is a shared foundation from where we all can unite upon.

Mosques, churches and synagogues are special places of prayer where the name of God is revered. In the Qur'an, God says that all these sanctuaries must be respected and preserved.

Rallying to a Common Formula

Concerning the People of the Book, God gives Muslims a command in the Qur'an; to rally to a common formula:

Say, "O People of the Book! Let us rally to a common formula to be binding on both us and you: That we worship none but God; that we associate no partners with Him; that we erect not, from among ourselves, Lords and patrons other than God." (Qur'an, 3:64)

This is indeed our call to Christians and Jews: As people who believe in God and follow His revelations, let us rally to a common formula – "faith". Let us love God, Who is our Creator and Lord, and follow His commands. And let us pray to God to lead us to an even straighter path.

When Muslims, Christians and Jews rally to a common formula this way; when they understand that they are friends not enemies, when they see that the real enemy is the rejection of God, then the world will become a very different place. The wars in many parts of the world, enmities, fears and

The evils in the world will come to an end when Muslims, Christians and Jews all worship God in unity, tolerating their differences of faith.

All Believers Must Pray For One Another and Be At Unity

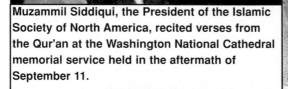

Muzammil Siddiqui, the President of the Islamic Society of North America, recited verses from the Qur'an at the Washington National Cathedral memorial service held in the aftermath of September 11.

Side: President Bush prayed next to a Muslim imam during a prayer service at the Washington National Cathedral. Above: Muslims and non-Muslims prayed together in a service in Dallas.

Bush's visit to the Islamic Center in Washingon.

After the attacks of September 11, people of every language and religion prayed to God in empathy and solidarity with the victims.

TIME, OCT, 1, 2001

PLANET EASTON, NOV, 2001

TERRORISM AND ISLAM ARE NOT THE SAME

Extremists representing a tiny fraction of Islam have caught the attention of the ... | inevitable clash of civilisations [...] Specifically, many believe there is an ...

LET US MOURN An interreligious ceremony at Bremen's Faith Mosque brings together leaders and adherents from Islam and Christianity to remember the victims of U.S. terror

TIME, OCT, 1, 2001

Q-NEWS, OCT, 2001

Bush and Blair:

Islam is peace, not terror

American people were appalled and outraged at last Tuesday's attacks. And so were Muslims all across the world. Both Americans and Muslim friends and citizens, tax-paying citizens, and Muslims in nations were just appalled and could not believe what we saw on our TV screens.

These acts of violence against innocents violate the fundamental tenets of the Islamic faith. And it's important for my fellow Americans to understand that.

The English translation is not as eloquent as the original Arabic, but let me quote from the Koran, itself: "In the long run, evil in the extreme will be the end of those who do evil. For that they rejected the signs of Allah and held them up to ridicule."

The face of terror is not the true faith of Islam. That's not what Islam is all about. Islam is peace. These terrorists don't represent peace. They represent evil and war.

Muslims in London's Hyde Park pray for victims of the attacks

TIME, OCT, 1, 2001

Karen Armstrong

The True, Peaceful Face of Islam

E ARE 1.2 BILLION MUSLIMS IN THE WORLD, AND ISLAM | an end as quickly as possible and must cease the min

terrorist attacks will come to an end, and a new civilisation based on love, respect and peace will be established upon this "common formula".

There are important facts to consider for Muslims. What God teaches us in the Qur'an about different peoples and creeds is clear:

* The morality of the Qur'an excludes every kind of racism.

* It is commanded in the Qur'an that, so long as they show no hostility to Islam or Muslims, a tolerant and friendly attitude must be maintained toward other religions.

Scenes of Respect: The Pope in a visit to the Wailing Wall in Jerusalem; European Union Commissioner Romano Prodi making a speech at the Islamic Centre in Brussels.

It is evident that the Jews have committed many errors which the Qur'an points out, criticizes and about which it gives a warning. The crimes committed by Israel in the present day against humanity are painfully well-known, but all this must not be taken by Muslims as a cause to feel hostility against all Jews. Again a basic vantage point prescribed by the Qur'an is not to make judgements about people just because they belong to a particular race, nation or religion. In every community, there are good people as well as wicked people. The Qur'an draws attention to this differentiation. For instance, right after mentioning the rebellious nature – against God and His religion – of some People of the Book, there is reference to an exception and, said thus:

> [However] They are not all alike. Among the People of the Book there is an upright community who recite the revelation of God during the night and fall prostrate before Him. They believe in God and the Last Day, enjoin what is right and forbid what is evil, and vie with one another in good works. They are of the righteous and whatever good

they do, its reward will not be denied them. God knows those who fear [Him]. (Qur'an 3:113-115)

In another verse, God commands:

We sent a Messenger among every people saying: "Worship God and keep clear of all false gods." Among them were some whom God guided but others received the misguidance they deserved. Travel about the earth and see the final fate of the deniers. (Qur'an, 16:36)

God revealed to all messengers that He is the Unique and that there is no one but Him whom people must worship, serve and obey. The divine message, conveyed to the people by God through His messengers, has been communicated to people since the creation of man. Some societies have accepted the message and followed the right path while others have denied and swerved from it. This also holds true for the present day. Some people will side with the righteous, whereas some others will plunge into mischief. This is the law of God. Those who believe should also adopt such an outlook and never forget that there may be sincere, pious people who have fear of God among the members of all religions as well as those who are far removed from the religious tenets.

Our hope is that a world will be established in which people will be able to live together in peace, no matter what race or religion they belong to, in which every racist perversion will be rejected, everyone's rights will be safeguarded and everyone will be respected. The struggle that will have to take place on intellectual grounds against all anti-religious ideologies will hopefully establish the peace that has been longed for. Of this God relates the following in the Qur'an:

Those who disbelieve are the friends and protectors of one another. If you do not act in this way (be friends and protectors of one another) there will be turmoil in the land and great corruption. (Qur'an, 8:73)

Would that there had been more people with a vestige of good among the generations of those who came before you, who forbade corruption in the earth, other than the few among them whom We saved. Those who did wrong gladly pursued the life of luxury that they were given and were evildoers. (Qur'an, 11:116)

Those who perform good actions will
receive better than them...
(Qur'an, 27:89)

ISLAM HAS BROUGHT PEACE AND HARMONY TO THE MIDDLE EAST

History always witnessed peace, justice and tolerance in the lands ruled by Muslim administrators when they followed Qur'anic guidance. The practices in the lands conquered during the lifetime of the Prophet Muhammad are very important examples, and just administrators succeeding him, who followed in the footsteps of God's messengers and never swerved from the morality of the Qur'an established peaceable societies. The true justice, righteousness and honesty described in the Qur'an persisted in the time of these administrators, thereby providing a role model for the succeeding generations to follow.

The land of Palestine and its capital Jerusalem, where members of the three divine religions reside together, are important in the sense that they show how Muslims bring peace and stability to the lands they rule. Indeed, for most of the last 1400 years, Muslim rule has brought peace to Jerusalem and Palestine.

The Peace and Justice Brought to Palestine by the Caliph Umar

Jerusalem was the capital of the Jews until A.D. 71. In that year, the Roman Army made a major assault on the Jews, and exiled them from the area with great savagery. As the time of the Jewish diaspora began, Jerusalem and the surrounding area was becoming an abandoned land.

However, Jerusalem once again became a centre of interest with the acceptance of Christianity during the time of the Roman Emperor Constantine. Roman Christians built churches in Jerusalem. The prohibitions on Jews settling in the region were lifted. Palestine remained Roman (Byzantine) territory up until the 7th century. The Persians conquered the region for a short time, but the Byzantines later reconquered it.

An important turning point in the history of Palestine came in the year 637, when it was conquered by the armies of Islam. This meant new peace and harmony in Palestine, which had for centuries been the scene of wars, exile, looting and massacre, and which saw new brutality every time it changed hands, a frequent occurrence. The coming of Islam was the beginning of an age when people of different beliefs could live in peace and harmony.

Palestine was captured by Umar, the second Caliph after the Prophet himself. The entry of the Caliph into Jerusalem, the tolerance, maturity and kindness he showed towards people of different beliefs, introduced the beautiful age that was beginning. The British historian and Middle East expert Karen Armstrong describes the capture of Jerusalem by Umar in these terms in her book *Holy War*:

The Caliph Omar entered Jerusalem mounted on a white camel, escorted by the magistrate of the city, the Greek Patriarch Sophronius. The Caliph asked to be taken immediately to the Temple Mount and there he knelt in prayer on the spot where his friend Mohammed had made his Night Journey. The Patriarch watched in horror: this, he thought, must be the Abomination of Desolation that the Prophet Daniel had foretold would enter the Temple; this must be Antichrist who would herald the Last Days. Next Omar asked to see the Christian shrines and, while he was in the Church of the Holy Sepulchre, the time for Muslim prayer came round. Courteously the Patriarch invited him to pray where he was, but Omar as courteously refused. **If he knelt to pray in the church, he explained, the Muslims would want to commemorate the event by erecting a mosque there, and that would mean that they would have to demolish the Holy Sepulchre.** Instead Omar went to pray at a little distance from the church, and, sure enough, directly opposite the Holy Sepulchre there is still a small mosque dedicated to the Caliph Omar.

The other great mosque of Omar was erected on the Temple Mount to

Mosque of Omar (also called Dome of the Rock)

mark the Muslim conquest, together with the mosque al-Aqsa which commemorates Mohammed's Night Journey. **For years, the Christians had used to the site of the ruined Jewish Temple as the city rubbish dump. The Caliph helped his Muslims to clear the garbage with his own hands** and there Muslims raised their two shrines to establish Islam in the third most holy city in the Islamic world.[21]

With the Muslim conquest of Jerusalem, the city became a safe haven in which all three religions could co-exist in peace. John L. Esposito writes:

When the Arab armies took Jerusalem in 638, they occupied a center whose shrines had made it a major pilgrimage site in Christendom. Churches and the Christian population were left unmolested. Jews, long banned from living there by Christian rulers, were permitted to return, live, and worship in the city of Solomon and David.[22]

When Caliph Umar entered Jerusalem, he signed the below agreement with the Patriarch of Jerusalem:

This is the security which 'Umar, the servant of God, the commander of the faithful, grants to the people of Ælia. He grants to all, whether sick or sound, security for their lives, their possessions, their churches and their crosses, and for all that concerns their religion. Their churches shall not be changed into dwelling places, nor destroyed, neither shall they nor their appurtenances be in any way diminished, nor the crosses of the inhabitants nor aught of their possessions, nor shall any constraint be put upon them in the matter of their faith, nor shall any one of them be harmed.[23]

In short, Muslims brought civilisation to Jerusalem and all of Palestine. Instead of beliefs that showed no respect for other peoples' sacred values, and which killed them simply out of differences of faith, there reigned the just, tolerant and moderate culture of Islam. After its capture by Umar, Muslims, Christians and Jews lived together in peace and harmony in Palestine. Muslims never tried to use force to make people convert, although some non-Muslims who saw that Islam was the true religion did so of their own free will.

The peace and harmony in Palestine lasted as long as Muslim rule in the region. However, at the end of the 11th century, a conquering force entered the region from

Under Muslim rule, Muslims, Christians and Jews lived together in Jerusalem in contentment, tolerance and peace.

The Muslims and Jews of Jerusalem were brutally massacred by the Crusaders.

abroad, and the civilised land of Jerusalem was barbarically and savagely plundered, in a way never before seen. These barbarians were the Crusaders.

The Savagery of the Crusaders

While members of all three religions were living peaceably together in Palestine, the Christians in Europe decided to organise a crusade. Following a call by Pope Urban II on 27 November 1095 at the Council of Clermont, more than 100,000 people from all over Europe set out for Palestine to free the Holy land from the Muslims and find the fabled wealth of the East. After a long and wearying journey, and much plundering and slaughter along the way, they reached Jerusalem in 1099. The city fell after a siege of nearly five weeks, and the Crusaders moved in. And they carried out a savagery the like of which the world has seldom seen. All Muslims and Jews in the city were put to the sword.

The peace and harmony in Palestine, which had lasted since Umar, ended in terrible slaughter. The Crusaders violated all the ethical laws of Christianity, a religion of love and compassion, and spread terror in the name of Christianity.

The Justice of Saladin

The barbaric Crusader army made Jerusalem their capital, and established a Latin Kingdom whose borders stretched from Palestine to Antioch. However, the Crusaders who brought savagery to Palestine did not last long. Saladin gathered all the Muslim kingdoms under his banner in a holy war, and defeated the Crusaders at the battle of Hattin in 1187. After the battle, the two leaders of the crusader army, Reynald of Chatillon and King Guy, were brought into Saladin's presence. Saladin executed Reynald of Chatillon, who had become infamous for the terrible savagery he had committed against Muslims, but he let King Guy go, as he had not committed the same crimes. Palestine once again saw the true meaning of justice.

Immediately after Hattin, and on the very same day that the Prophet Muhammad had been taken from Mecca to Jerusalem in one night, the day of the Ascent, Saladin entered Jerusalem and freed it from 88 years of Crusader occupation. When the Crusaders took the city 88 years earlier, they killed all the Muslims inside it, and for that reason they were afraid that Saladin would do the same thing to them. However, he did not touch even one Christian in the city. Furthermore, he merely ordered the Latin (Catholic) Christians to leave it. The Orthodox Christians, who were not Crusaders, were allowed to live in the city and worship as they chose. In the words of John L. Esposito, "The Muslim army was as magnanimous in victory as it had been tenacious in battle. Civilians were spared; churches and shrines were generally left untouched... Saladin was faithful to his word and compassionate toward noncombatants." [24]

Karen Armstrong describes the second capture of Jerusalem in these words:

On 2 October 1187 Saladin and his army entered Jerusalem as conquerors and for the next 800 years Jerusalem would remain a Muslim city. Saladin kept his word, and conquered the city according to the highest Islamic ideals. **He did not take revenge for the 1099 massacre, as the Qur'an advised (16:127), and now that hostilities had ceased he ended the killing (2:193-194).** Not a single Christian was killed and there was no plunder. The ransoms were deliberately very low... Saladin was moved to tears by the plight of families who were rent asunder and he released many of them freely, as the Qur'an urged, though to the despair of his long-suffering treasurers. His brother al-Adil was so distressed by the plight of the prisoners that he asked Saladin for a thousand of them for his own use and then released them on the spot... All the Muslim leaders were scandalised to see the rich Christians escaping with their wealth, which could have been used to ransom all the prisoners... [The Patriarch] Heraclius paid his ten-dinar ransom like everybody else and was even provided with a special escort to keep his treasure safe during the journey to Tyre.[25]

In short, Saladin and the Muslims in his command treated the Christians with great mercy and justice, and even showed them more compassion than their own leaders had. Not only the Christians but also Jews attained peace and security with the conquest of Jerusalem by Muslims. The well-known Spanish-Jewish poet Yehuda al-Harizi expressed his feelings thus in one of his works:

God ...decided that the sanctuary would no longer rest in the hands of the sons of Esau... Thus in the year 4950 of Creation [AD 1190] God aroused the spirit of the prince of the Ishmaelites [Salah al-Din], a prudent and courageous man, who came with his entire army, besieged Jerusalem, took it and had it proclaimed throughout the country that he would receive and accept the race of Ephraim, wherever they came from. And so we came from all corners of the world to take up residence here. We now live in the shadow of peace.[26]

After Jerusalem, the Crusaders continued their barbarity and the Muslims their justice in other cities in Palestine. In 1194, Richard the Lionheart, who is portrayed as a great hero in British history, had 3,000 Muslims, among whom were many women and children, basely executed in Castle Acre. Although the Muslims witnessed this savagery, they never resorted to the same methods. They abided by God's command **"Let not the hatred of a people [who once] obstructed you from the Sacred Mosque lead you to transgress..."** (Qur'an, 5:2) and never used violence against innocent civilians. They never employed unnecessary violence, not even against the Crusader armies they defeated.

The savagery of the Crusaders and the justice of the Muslims once more revealed a historic truth: **An administration built on the principles of Islam**

King Richard ruthlessly executed 3000 Muslim civilians in the Castle of Acre, among whom were many women and children.

allowed people of different faiths to live together. This fact continued to be demonstrated for 700 years after Saladin, particularly during the Ottoman period.

The Ottoman Empire's Just and Tolerant Rule

In 1514, Sultan Selim captured Jerusalem and the surrounding area, and some 400 years of Ottoman rule in Palestine began. As in other Ottoman states, this period would enable Palestine to enjoy peace, stability, and the living together of different faiths.

The Ottoman Empire was administered under what is known as the **"nation (millet) system"**, the fundamental feature of which was that people of different faiths were allowed to live according to their own beliefs and even legal systems. Christians and Jews, described as the People of the Book in the Qur'an, found tolerance, security and freedom in Ottoman lands.

The most important reason for this was that although the Ottoman Empire was an Islamic state administered by Muslims, it had no desire to force its citizens to adopt Islam. On the contrary, the Ottoman state aimed at providing

Although the Ottoman Empire was a Muslim state, it granted its subjects religious freedom. Thus a peaceful multi-cultural mosaic was to be found in Ottoman lands. As seen in this picture, the state protected its citizens in accordance with Muslim moral teaching, providing for its poor no matter what religion they practised.

The mutual intolerance of Catholics and Protestants in the 16th and 17th centuries still continues in some countries. The most innocent victims of these conflicts have always been the children.

peace and security for non-Muslims, and governing them in such a way that they would be pleased with Islamic rule and justice.

Other major states at the same time had much cruder, oppressive and intolerant views of government. The Kingdom of Spain could not tolerate the existence of Muslims and Jews on the Spanish peninsula and inflicted great violence on both communities. In many other European countries, Jews were oppressed just for being Jews (for instance they were imprisoned in ghettoes), and were sometimes the victims of mass slaughter (pogroms). Christians could not even get on with one another: the fighting between Protestants and Catholics in the 16th and 17th centuries turned Europe into a bloodbath. The 30-Years War between 1618 and 1648 was one result of this Catholic-Protestant conflict. As a result of that war, central Europe became a battleground, and in Germany alone, one-third of the population of 15 million people was killed.

The Ottoman Solution to Jerusalem — ZAMAN, 30.8.00

Kudüs'e Osmanlı çözümü

Nostalgia for the Ottomans in the Balkans

We Miss the Ottomans — TÜRKİYE, 15.4.95

Arap Dünyası, medeniyetin, hoşgörünün ve adaletin baş tacı edildiği dönemin özlemi içinde

Osmanlı'yı arıyoruz

Mısır'ın tarih araştı... son yıllarda

Araştırma-İnceleme

Onu sadece Müslümanlar değil Hristiyanlar da özlüyor...

Balkanlar Osmanlı'ya hasret!

Yunanlı yazar Michel de Greece şunları söylemektedir: "Osmanlı Devleti'nin yıkılmasından çok üzüntü

Osmanlı gitti terör başladı

Terörün kaynağı Balfour deklarasyonuna uzanıyor. Osmanlı'nın yıkılmasının ardından bölgede birçok aile devleti kuruldu. Daha sonra İsrail devleti kuruldu. Filistin İsrail arasındaki çatışmalarda 35 bin mas... Filistinli öldü. Bugün Amerika'yı oluşturan üç büyük dindeki hangi insana sorarsanız

Ottomans Departed and Terror Started

The model for peace in the Middle East is the Ottoman one of multi-culturalism, with its conciliatory, just and tolerant attitude based on the moral teaching of the Qur'an. Above are some news clippings from Turkish newspapers and journals about the peaceful nature of Ottoman rule.

In such an environment, it is an indisputably important truth that Ottoman rule was exceedingly humane.

Many historians and political scientists have drawn attention to this fact. One of these is Columbia University's world-famous Middle East expert Professor Edward Said. Originally from a Jerusalem Christian family, he continues his research far from his homeland in American universities. In an interview in the Israeli newspaper Ha'aretz he recommended the "**Ottoman nation system**" if a permanent peace is to be built in the Middle East. What he said was:

A Jewish minority can survive the way other minorities in the Arab world

A widely-recognized expert on the Middle East, Edward W. Said

survived. ...it worked rather well under the Ottoman Empire, with its millet system. What they had then seems a lot more humane than what we have now.[27]

History reveals that Islam is the only system of belief to offer a just, tolerant and compassionate way of government in the Middle East. The Pax Ottomana, which came to an end with the withdrawal of the Ottoman Empire from the region, has still not been replaced.

For this reason, the way to attain peace in the Middle East is to introduce the Ottoman model characterised by tolerance and compromise, the two fundamental teachings of the Qur'an. Islam, truly followed, is the solution to all sorts of violence of all kinds, conflicts, wars and terror and a guarantor of peace, justice and tolerance.

God is Ever-Gentle with His servants.
(Qur'an, 3:30)

God is Ever-Gentle with His servants.
(Qur'an, 3:30)

THE REAL ROOTS OF TERRORISM: DARWINISM AND MATERIALISM

Most people think the theory of evolution was first proposed by Charles Darwin, and rests on scientific evidence, observations and experiments. However, the truth is that Darwin was not its originator, neither does the theory rest on scientific proof. The theory consists of an adaptation to nature of the ancient dogma of materialist philosophy. Although it is not backed up by scientific discoveries, the theory is blindly supported in the name of materialist philosophy. (see Harun Yahya, *The Evolution Deceit*, Taha Publishers, 1999)

This fanaticism has resulted in all kinds of disasters. Together with the spread of Darwinism and the materialist philosophy it supports, the answer to the question "What is a human being?" has changed. People who used to answer: "Human beings were created by God and have to live according to the beautiful morality He teaches", have now begun to think that "Man came into being by chance, and is an animal who developed by means of the fight for survival." There is a heavy price to pay for this great deception. Violent ideologies such as racism, fascism and communism, and many other barbaric world views based on conflict have all drawn strength from this deception.

This part of the book will examine the disaster Darwinism has visited on the world and reveal its connection with terrorism, one of the most important global problems of our time.

The Darwinist Lie: "Life is Conflict"

Darwin set out with one basic premise when developing his theory: **The development of living things depends on the fight for survival. The strong win the struggle. The weak are condemned to defeat and oblivion.**

According to Darwin, there is a ruthless struggle for survival and an eternal conflict in nature. The strong always overcome the weak, and this enables development to take place. The subtitle he gave to his book *The Origin of Species*, *"The Origin of Species by Means of Natural Selection or the Preservation of Favoured Races in the Struggle for Life"*, encapsulates that view.

Furthermore, Darwin proposed that the "fight for survival" also applied between human racial groups. According to that mythical claim, favoured races were victorious in the struggle. Favoured races, in Darwin's view, were white Europeans. African or Asian races had lagged behind in the struggle for survival. Darwin went further, and suggested that these races would soon lose the struggle for survival entirely, and thus disappear:

> At some future period, not very distant as measured by centuries, the civilised races of man will almost certainly exterminate and replace the savage races throughout the world. At the same time the anthropomorphous apes … will no doubt be exterminated. The break

between man and his nearest allies will then be wider, for it will intervene between man in a more civilised state, as we may hope, **even than the Caucasian, and some ape as low as a baboon, instead of as now between the negro or Australian and the gorilla.**[28]

The Indian anthropologist Lalita Vidyarthi explains how Darwin's theory of evolution imposed racism on the social sciences:

> **His (Darwin's) theory of the survival of the fittest** was warmly welcomed by the social scientists of the day, and they believed mankind had achieved various levels of evolution culminating in the white man's civilization. **By the second half of the nineteenth century racism was accepted as fact by the vast majority of Western scientists.**[29]

Darwin's Source of Inspiration: Malthus's Theory of Ruthlessness

Darwin's source of inspiration on this subject was the British economist Thomas Malthus's book A*n Essay on the Principle of Population.* Left to their own devices, Malthus calculated that the human population increased rapidly. In his view, the main influences that kept populations under control were disasters such as war, famine and disease. In short, according to this brutal claim, some people had to die for others to live. Existence came to mean permanent war.

In the 19th century, Malthus's ideas were widely accepted. European upper class intellectuals in particular supported his cruel ideas. In the article **"The Scientific Background of the Nazi "Race Purification" Programme,"** by Jerry Bergman, the importance 19th century Europe attached to Malthus's

Thomas Malthus

views on population is described in this way:

> In the opening half of the nineteenth century, throughout Europe, members of the ruling classes gathered to discuss the newly discovered "Population problem" and to devise ways of implementing the Malthusian mandate, to increase the mortality rate of the poor: **"Instead of recommending cleanliness to the poor, we should encourage contrary habits. In our towns we should make the streets narrower, crowd more people into the houses, and court the return of the plague. In the country we should build our villages near stagnant pools, and particularly encourage settlements in all marshy and unwholesome situations,"** and so forth and so on.[30]

As a result of this cruel policy, the weak, and those who lost the struggle for survival would be eliminated, and as a result the rapid rise in population would be balanced out. This so-called "oppression of the poor" policy was

The implementation in the 19th century of Malthus's thesis of the necessity of the struggle for life brought misery to the helpless and poor children in England. Religion, however, ensures the protection of children. A life of goodness and virtue, without any misery and suffering, is only possible if the moral teachings of religion are practiced.

actually carried out in 19th century Britain. An industrial order was set up in which children of eight and nine were made to work sixteen hours a day in the coal mines and thousands died from the terrible conditions. The struggle for survival demanded by Malthus's theory led to millions of Britons leading lives full of suffering.

Influenced by these ideas, Darwin applied this concept of conflict to all of nature, and proposed that the strong and the fittest emerged victorious from this war of existence. Moreover, he claimed that the so-called struggle for survival was a justified and unchangeable law of nature. On the other hand, he invited people to abandon their religious beliefs by denying the Creation, and thus undermined all ethical values that might prove to be obstacles to the ruthlessness of the struggle for survival.

Humanity has paid a heavy price in the 20th century for the dissemination of these callous views which led people to ruthlessness and cruelty.

The Role of Darwinism in Preparing the Ground for World War I

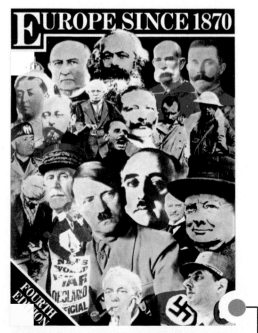

Europe Since 1870 by the English professor of history, James Joll.

As Darwinism dominated European culture, the effects of the struggle for survival began to emerge. Colonialist European nations in particular began to portray the nations they colonized as **"evolutionary backward nations"** and looked to Darwinism for justification.

The bloodiest political effect of Darwinism was the outbreak of World War I in 1914.

In his book *Europe Since 1870*, the well-known British professor of history James Joll explains that one of the factors that prepared the ground for World War I was the belief in Darwinism of European rulers at the time.

...it is important to realise how literally the doctrine of the struggle for existence and of the survival of the fittest was taken by the majority of the leaders of Europe in the years preceding the First World War. The Austro-Hungarian chief of staff for example, Franz Baron Conrad von Hoetzendorff, wrote in his memoirs after the war:

Philanthropic religions, moral teachings and philosophical doctrines may certainly sometimes serve to **weaken mankind's struggle for existence** in its crudest form, but they will never succeed in removing it as a driving motive of the world... **It is in accordance with this great principle that the catastrophe of the world war came about as the result of the motive forces in the lives of states and peoples, like a thunderstorm which must by its nature discharge itself.**

Seen against this sort of ideological background, Conrad's insistence on the need for a preventive war in order to preserve the Austro-Hungarian monarchy becomes comprehensible.

We have seen too how these views were not limited to military figures, and that Max Weber for example was deeply concerned with the international struggle for survival. Again Kurt Riezler, the personal assistant and confidant of the German chancellor Theobald von Bethmann-Hollweg, wrote in 1914:

Eternal and absolute enmity is fundamentally inherent in relations between peoples; and **the hostility which we observe everywhere**... is not the result of a perversion of human nature but is **the essence of the world and the source of life itself.**[31]

Friedrich von Bernardi, a World War I general, made a similar connection between war and the laws of war in nature. **"War"** declared Bernhardi **"is a biological necessity"**; it "is as necessary as the struggle of the elements of nature"; it "gives a biologically just decision, since its decisions rest on the very nature of things."[32]

As we have seen, World War I broke out because of European thinkers, generals and administrators who saw warfare, bloodshed and suffering as a

European philosophers and political leaders of the first decade of the 20th century were obsessed with the Darwinist notion of "the struggle for existence". Hence their enthusiasm for starting the Great War, a terrible cataclysm that destroyed more than 10 million lives.

kind of development, and thought they were an unchanging law of nature. The ideological root that dragged all of that generation to destruction was nothing else than Darwin's concepts of the "struggle for survival" and "favoured races." World War I left behind it 8 million dead, hundreds of ruined cities, and millions of wounded, crippled, homeless and unemployed.

The basic cause of World War II, which broke out 21 years later and left 55 million dead behind it, was also based on Darwinism.

What "The Law of the Jungle" Led to: Fascism

As Darwinism fed racism in the 19th century, it formed the basis of an ideology that would develop and drown the world in blood in the 20th century: Nazism.

A strong Darwinist influence can be seen in Nazi ideologues. When one examines this theory, which was

Fascism, which has Darwinist concepts at its heart, caused the death of millions of innocent people. This dreadful ideology drew many countries of the world into a maelstrom of destruction and misery.

given shape by Adolf Hitler and Alfred Rosenberg, one comes across such concepts as "natural selection," "selective mating," and "the struggle for survival between the races," which are repeated dozens of time in the works of Darwin. When calling his book *Mein Kampf* (My Struggle), Hitler was inspired by the Darwinist struggle for survival and the principle that victory went to the fittest. He particularly talks about the struggle between the races:

> History would culminate in a new millennial empire of unparalleled splendour, based on a new racial hierarchy ordained by nature herself.[33]

> In the 1933 Nuremberg party rally, Hitler proclaimed that "a higher race subjects to itself a lower race… a right which we see in nature and which can be regarded as the sole conceivable right". [34]

That the Nazis were influenced by Darwinism is a fact that almost all historians who are expert in the matter accept. Peter Chrisp, the author of the book, *The Rise of Fascism*, expressed this fact as follows:

> Charles Darwin's theory that humans had evolved from apes was ridiculed when it was first published, but was later widely accepted. The Nazis distorted Darwin's theories, using them to justify warfare and racism.[35]

The historian Hickman describes Darwinism's influence on Hitler as follows: (Hitler) was a firm believer and preacher of evolution. Whatever the deeper, profound, complexities of his psychosis, it is certain that [the concept of struggle was important because] … his book, Mein Kampf, clearly set forth a number of evolutionary ideas, particularly those emphasizing struggle, survival of the fittest and the extermination of the weak to produce a better society.[36]

Hitler, who emerged with these views,

Nazism, a blend of Social Darwinism and neo-paganism, has killed millions and spread horror into the hearts of many others.

World War II caused the deaths of 55 million people, leaving many others wounded and homeless, their lives in ruins. The war devastated cities and caused economies to collapse.

dragged the world to violence that had never before been seen. Many ethnic and political groups, and especially the Jews, were exposed to terrible cruelty and slaughter in the Nazi concentration camps. World War II, which began with the Nazi invasion, cost 55 million lives. What lay behind the greatest tragedy in world history was Darwinism's concept of the "struggle for survival."

The Bloody Alliance: Darwinism and Communism

While fascists are found on the right wing of Social Darwinism, the left wing is occupied by communists. Communists have always been among the fiercest defenders of Darwin's theory.

This relationship between Darwinism and communism goes right back to the founders of both these "isms." Marx and Engels, the founders of communism, read Darwin's *The Origin of Species* as soon as it came out, and were amazed at its dialectical materialist attitude. The correspondence between Marx and Engels showed that they saw Darwin's theory as "containing the basis in natural history for communism." In his book *The Dialectics of Nature*, which he wrote under the influence of Darwin, Engels was full of praise for Darwin, and tried to make his own contribution to the theory in the chapter "The Part Played by Labour in the Transition from Ape to Man."

Russian communists who followed in the footsteps of Marx and Engels, such as Plekhanov, Lenin, Trotsky and Stalin, all agreed with Darwin's theory of evolution. Plekhanov, who is seen as the founder of Russian communism, regarded Marxism as **"Darwinism in its application to social science."**[37]

Trotsky said, **"Darwin's discovery is the highest triumph of the dialectic in the whole field of organic matter."**[38]

Darwinist education had a major role in the formation of communist cadres. For instance, historians note the fact that **Stalin was religious in his youth, but became an atheist primarily because of Darwin's books.**

Mao, who established communist rule in China and killed millions of people, openly stated that **"Chinese socialism is founded upon Darwin and the theory of evolution."**[39]

The Harvard University historian James Reeve Pusey goes into great

Communist leaders, whose ideas of human society were also based on Darwinism, will go down in history as having caused terrible suffering with their cruel policies.

detail regarding Darwinism's effect on Mao and Chinese communism in his research book *China and Charles Darwin*.

In short, there is an unbreakable link between the theory of evolution and communism. The theory claims that living things are the product of chance, and provides a so-called scientific support for atheism. Communism, an atheist ideology, is for that reason firmly tied to Darwinism. Moreover, the theory of evolution proposes that development in nature is possible thanks to conflict (in other words "the struggle for survival") and supports the concept of "dialectics" which is fundamental to communism.

If we think of the communist concept of "dialectical conflict," which killed some 120 million people during the 20th century, as a "killing machine", then we can better understand the dimensions of the disaster that Darwinism visited on the planet.

Communism applied the Darwinian idea of conflict to the class conflict, and thus accepted murder and bloodshed as legitimate methods of control.

Dialectical Conflict Does Not Foster the Development of Societies, It Destroys Them

As we learned earlier, Darwinism proposed that the struggle between living things is the cause of their development and gained so-called scientific currency for the philosophy of dialectical materialism.

As can be understood from its name, dialectical materialism rests on the idea of "conflict". Karl Marx, the founder of this philosophy, propagated the idea that **"if there were no struggle and opposition, everything would stay as it is."** In another place he said, **"Force is the midwife of every old society pregnant with a new one."**[40] By saying this, he called people to violence, war and bloodshed in order that they could develop.

The first to apply Marx's theory in the realm of politics was Lenin. Fostering the idea that **"progress comes about as a result of the conflict of opposites"**, Lenin advocated that people with opposing ideas should be in constant conflict. Lenin also repeatedly stated that this conflict would require bloodshed, that is, terrorism. A piece by Lenin titled "Guerrilla Warfare" which was first published in *Proletary* in 1906, eleven years before the Bolshevik Revolution, shows the terrorist methods he had adopted:

> **The phenomenon in which we are interested is the armed struggle.** It is conducted by individuals and by small groups. Some belong to revolutionary organisations, while others (the majority in certain parts of Russia) do not belong to any revolutionary organisation. Armed struggle pursues two different aims, which must be strictly distinguished: in the first place, **this struggle aims at assassinating individuals, chiefs and subordinates in the Army and police; in the second place, it aims at the confiscation of monetary funds both from the government and from private persons.** The confiscated funds go partly into the treasury of the party, partly for the special purpose of arming and preparing for an uprising, and partly for the maintenance of persons engaged in the struggle we are describing. [41]

In the twentieth century, one of the most well known ideologies to oppose communism was fascism. The interesting thing is that, although fascism declared itself opposed to communism, it believed just as much as communism in the concept of struggle. Communists believed in the necessity of the class struggle; the fascists simply changed the arena of the struggle concentrating on the idea of the struggle between races and nations. For example, the German historian Heinrich Treitschke, one of the most important sources for Nazi ideas and a prominent racist, wrote, **"nations could not prosper without intense competition, like the struggle for survival of Darwin."**[42] Hitler also said that he had taken inspiration from Darwin's understanding of struggle:

> **The whole world of Nature is a mighty struggle between strength and weakness—an eternal victory of the strong over the weak.** There would be nothing but decay in the whole of nature if this were not so. He who would live must fight. He who does not wish to fight in this world where permanent struggle is the law of life, has not the right to exist.[43]

These two social Darwinist ideologies believed that, for a society to grow strong, struggle and bloodshed are necessary; what they created in the 20th century is well known. Countless numbers of innocent people died; countless others were wounded or maimed; national economies crumbled; money that used to be spent on health, research, technology, education and art was spent on arms, on bandages to bind the wounds caused by those arms and to restore ruined cities. It became evident as time went on that struggle and terror did not to promote human development but rather destruction.

Certainly there are contradictions in the world. Just as in nature there are light and darkness, day and night, hot and cold, so there are also contradictions in putting ideas into practice. But a contradiction in ideas does not necessitate conflict. On the contrary, if contradictions are approached with tolerance, peace, understanding, love, compassion and mercy, good results may be achieved. Everyone who compares his own idea with another's may develop his own or see its deficiencies and remedy them. Those who defend opposing opinions could have an exchange of ideas in conversation or engage in a constructive critique. Only the kind of sincere, forgiving, peaceful and humble person who conforms to the moral teaching of the Qur'an can develop this approach.

To kill a person or do him harm because he has different ideas, believes in a different religion or belongs to a different race is an immense act of cruelty. For this reason only, throughout history and all over the world, sons and

It is natural that disagreements occur, but they should not be the cause of conflict and wars between people. Mutual respect and tolerance can ensure agreement and co-existence between parties in disagreement. The moral teaching of the Qur'an offers to people a life of contentment and joy, whereas the dialectical struggle always brings unhappiness, destruction and death.

daughters of the same fatherland have struggled with one another to the death, murdering one another without pity. Or people of different race or nationality, women and children included, have been indiscriminately slaughtered. The only person who could do such a thing is someone who has no respect for a human being, and who regards the person in front of him just as an intelligent animal; it is someone who does not believe that he will have to give an account to God for what he has done.

The best and truest attitude to have towards opposing ideas is revealed in the Qur'an. Clashes of ideas have arisen throughout history and one of the most well-known examples of this is the opposition between Moses and his contemporary Pharaoh. Despite all Pharaoh's cruelty and aggressiveness, God sent Moses to invite him to God's religion, and He explained the method Moses was to use:

> **Go to Pharaoh; he has overstepped the bounds. But speak to him with gentle words so that hopefully he will pay heed or show some fear. (Qur'an, 20:43-44)**

Moses obeyed God's command and explained true religion to him at great length. In order to stop Pharaoh's denial of God and his cruelty to people, Moses patiently explained every matter. However, Pharaoh showed a hostile attitude toward Moses' noble character and patience, threatening to kill him and those who shared his ideas. But it was not Pharaoh's attitude that prevailed; on the contrary, he and his people were drowned. Moses and his people were victorious.

As this example shows, the victory of an idea or the struggle for development does not come about by hostility or aggression. The meeting between Moses and Pharaoh offers a lesson from history: it is not those on the side of contention and cruelty who are victorious, but those who are on the side of peace and justice. The exercise of fine moral principles receives its reward both in this world and in the hereafter

Darwinism and Terrorism

As we have so far seen, Darwinism is at the root of various ideologies of violence that have spelled disaster to mankind in the 20th century. The fundamental concept behind this understanding and method is **"fighting whoever is not one of us."** There are different beliefs, worldviews and philosophies in the world. It is very natural that all these diverse ideas have traits opposing one another. However, these different stances can look at each other in one of two ways:

1) They can respect the existence of those who are not like them and try to establish dialogue with them, employing a humane method. Indeed, this method conforms with the morality of the Qur'an.

2) They can choose to fight others, and to try to secure an advantage by damaging them, in other words, to behave like a wild animal. This is a method employed by materialism, that is, irreligion.

The horror we call "terrorism" is nothing other than a statement of the second view.

When we consider the difference between these two approaches, we can see that the idea of **"man as a fighting animal"** which Darwinism has subconsciously imposed on people is particularly influential. Individuals and

There may be disagreement between states or societies, but conflict and war can never solve the problems. As the Qur'an teaches, all disagreements must be solved by mutual patience, tolerance, compassion and understanding.

groups who choose the way of conflict may never have heard of Darwinism and the principles of that ideology. But at the end of the day they agree with a view whose philosophical basis rests on Darwinism. What leads them to believe in the rightness of this view is such Darwinism-based slogans as "In this world, the strong survive," "Big fish swallow little ones," "War is a virtue," and "Man advances by waging war." Take Darwinism away, and these are nothing but empty slogans.

Actually, when Darwinism is taken away, no philosophy of conflict remains. The three divine religions that most people in the world believe in, Islam, Christianity and Judaism, all oppose violence. All three religions wish to bring peace and harmony to the world, and oppose innocent people being killed and suffering cruelty and torture. Conflict and violence violate the morality that God has set out for man, and are abnormal and unwanted concepts. However, Darwinism sees and portrays conflict and violence as

The only way for future generations to ensure for themselves a virtuous and contented life is the moral teachings of the Qur'an.

natural, justified and correct concepts that have to exist.

For this reason, if some people commit terrorism using the concepts and symbols of Islam, Christianity or Judaism in the name of those religions, you can be sure that those people are not Muslims, Christians or Jews. They are real Social Darwinists. They hide under a cloak of religion, but they are not genuine believers. Even if they claim to be serving religion, they are actually enemies of religion and of believers. That is because they are ruthlessly committing a crime that religion forbids, and in such a way as to blacken religion in peoples' eyes.

For this reason, the root of the terrorism that plagues our planet is not in any of the divine religions, but in atheism, and the expression of atheism in our times: Darwinism and materialism.

Every Person Who Desires Peace Must Recognise the Danger of Darwinism

The solution in the fight against a particular problem lies in doing away with the ideas this problem fundamentally depends on. For instance, no matter how hard one endeavours to keep the surroundings of a stinking garbage bin clean, the garbage will keep on stinking. All solutions will prove to be short-lived. The real solution lies in a thorough cleaning of the garbage's source, removing the trash altogether. Alternatively, this is like spending years raising poisonous snakes on a farm, then letting them go, wondering why they start to bite people and trying to round them all up again. The important thing is not to breed them in the first place.

Consequently, in the fight against terrorism, searching for terrorists one by one and trying to render them ineffectual does not provide a viable and permanent solution. **The only way of totally eradicating the scourge of terrorism from the face of the earth is to identify the basic sources that breed terrorists and remove them. The main source of terrorism, on the other hand, is erroneous ideologies and the education received in the light of these ideologies.**

In our day, in almost all countries of the world, Darwinism is incorporated into school curricula and is considered to be scientific fact. Young people are

God commands justice and doing good and giving to relatives. And He forbids indecency and doing wrong and tyranny...
(Qur'an, 16:90)

not taught that they are created by God, that they are endowed with a spirit, wisdom and conscience. They are not told that they will have to give account of their deeds on the Day of Judgement and accordingly be punished in hell or rewarded with paradise for all eternity. On the contrary, they are taught that they are creatures whose forefathers were animals that somehow came into existence by some random coincidences. Under such indoctrination, they assume themselves to be stray beings who are not answerable to God and see their future – that is their survival – in being victorious through struggle. After this stage, it becomes rather easy to brainwash these people, who have been already indoctrinated all through their school lives, and to turn them into enemies of humanity cruel enough to murder innocent children. Such young people can be readily attracted by any strayed ideology; they can act under the influence of the terrorists' conditioning and engage in inconceivably cruel and violent acts. The communist, fascist and racist terrorist groups that have been in existence since the 19th century are the products of this kind of education system.

The second great harm this education system does is to entirely distance education from religion, thereby limiting the sphere of religion to the world of uneducated people. Thus, while those who have access to education are totally removed from religion thanks to Darwinist-materialist instillation, religion becomes something peculiar to the uneducated. This causes the development of superstitious and erroneous ideas and allows those who put forward ideas totally contrary to religion in the name of religion to take control easily.

The recent events of September 11 are the most obvious examples of this. No one who fears God, loves Him and expects to give an account of his deeds in the hereafter can commit any act that will leave thousands of innocent people dead or wounded and orphan thousands of children. Such a person knows that he will give an account to God for every person he subjected to cruelty and each one of them will become a source of anguish for him in hell.

To conclude, the way to stop acts of terrorism is to put an end to Darwinist-materialist education, to educate young people in accord with a curricula based on true scientific findings and to instil in them the fear of God and the desire to act wisely and scrupulously. The fruits of such an education will be a community made up of peaceable, trustworthy, forgiving and tolerant people.

It is He who sends down Clear
Signs to His servant to bring you out of the
darkness to the light. (Qur'an, 57:9)

CONCLUSION: RECOMMENDATIONS TO THE WESTERN WORLD AND MUSLIMS

T oday, the Western world is concerned about the organisations that use terror under the guise of Islam and this concern is not misplaced. It is obvious that those carrying out terror and their supporters should be tried according to international judicial criteria. However, a more important point to consider is the long-term strategies that have to be pursued to discover viable solutions to these problems.

The assessments above reveal that terror has no place in Islam and that it is a crime committed against humanity. They further show the inherently contradictory nature of the concept of "Islamic terror". This provides us with an important vantage point:

1) The time ahead requires all countries to act with caution, sensitivity and wisdom. The bleak scenario that unfolds with the "Clash of civilisations", is one to the detriment of the whole world, and from which no one benefits. The world community at large must take the opportunity to learn to live side by side in peaceful interchange, learning from each other, studying each other's history, accomplishments in religion, art, literature, philosophy, science, technology, and culture, all of which mutually enrich one another's lives.

2) **The activities serving the presentation of true Islam must be widespread.** The solution to combat radical factions in Islamic countries should not be "compulsory secularisation". On the contrary, such a policy will incite more reaction from the masses. The solution is the dissemination of true Islam and the appearance of a Muslim model which embraces the Qur'anic values such as human rights, democracy, freedom, high morality, science, spirituality, aesthetics, and which offers happiness and bliss to humanity. Muslims must explain and live by the moral values commanded by the Qur'an and as exemplified by Muhammad, the Messenger of God. Muslims have the responsibility to take Islam out from the hands of those who misapply it, (which leads to further misunderstanding of Islam) and place it back into the hands of those who live by the teachings of Islamic virtue and by the example of Muhammad, the Messenger of God.

3) The source of terrorism is in ignorance and bigotry and the solution to terrorism is education. To the circles who feel sympathy with terror, it should be made clear that terror is utterly against Islam and that it only serves to harm Islam, Muslims and humanity at large.

4) Long-term cultural solutions must be devised to combat terrorism which has its roots in communist, fascist and racist ideologies. Today in countries all over the world, Darwinist precepts form the basis of the education system. However, as we have stressed earlier, Darwinism is an erroneous ideology that sees man as an animal who developed only by fighting for survival – something which constitutes the likely basis of all forms of terrorism. An ideology that predicts only those holding power will survive and considers war as a virtue is like a huge morass that will never cease to visit

disaster on the world. This being the case, beside the judicial and other measures that will be introduced to combat terrorism, there is also a need for a vigorous education campaign to be launched all over the world. Disclosure of the real face of the deception of Darwinism and materialism and instruction in the good values God has revealed for people must be the fundamentals of this education. Peace and stability are attainable only through living by the good values of true religion. Without draining the morass, it is not possible to rid the world of disaster.

Our hope is that these measures will help to the world get rid of terrorism and all other bigoted, brutal, barbarous structures. With the Christian culture it represents, since the United States defines itself as "a nation under God", it should be a friend of the Muslims. In the Qur'an, God draws attention to this fact and informs us that Christians are those who are **"most affectionate to those who believe"**. (Qur'an, 5:82)

In history, some ignorant people (for instance, the Crusaders) failed to understand this fact and caused conflicts between these two religions. To prevent the repetition of this scenario, which is propagated with mottos like "Clash of Civilizations" or "Holy War against the West", true Christians and Muslims need to come together and co-operate.

Indeed, the developments which took place in the aftermath of these grievous events indicate that the seeds of this co-operation has already been sowed. This grave act of terrorism, which has drawn the Christian and Muslim communities closer, led many Christians come to know more about the religion of Islam and encouraged Muslims to make greater efforts to communicate true Islamic morality described in the Qur'an.

All these developments are the glad tidings that people will understand Islamic values better and be able to rid themselves of any prejudices they had held. By the Will of God, the 21st century will be the time when people will truly acknowledge that the dissemination of the values of Islam is the unique way of achieving much longed-for peace on the planet.

He is God - the Creator, the
Maker, the Giver of Form...
(Qu'ran, 59:24)

THE MISCONCEPTION OF EVOLUTION

Darwinism, which seeks to deny the fact of creation in the universe, is nothing but an unscientific fallacy. This theory, which argues that life originated from inanimate matter through coincidences, has been demolished with the recognition that the universe was created by God. It is God Who created the universe and Who designed it down to its smallest detail. Therefore, it is impossible for the theory of evolution, which holds that living beings are not created by God, but are products of coincidences, to be true.

Unsurprisingly, when we look at the theory of evolution, we see that this theory is denounced by scientific findings. The design in life is extremely complex and striking. In the inanimate world, for instance, we can explore how sensitive are the balances which atoms rest upon, and further, in the animate world, we can observe in what complex designs these atoms were brought together, and how extraordinary are the mechanisms and structures such as proteins, enzymes, and cells, which are manufactured with them.

This extraordinary design in life invalidated Darwinism at the end of the 20th century.

We have dealt with this subject in great detail in some of our other studies, and shall continue to do so. However, we think that, considering its importance, it will be helpful to make a short summary here as well.

Charles Darwin

The Scientific Collapse of Darwinism

Although a doctrine going back as far as ancient Greece, the theory of evolution was advanced extensively in the 19th century. The most important development that made the theory the top topic of the world of science was the book by Charles Darwin titled *"The Origin of Species"* published in 1859. In this book, Darwin denied that different living species on the earth were created separately by God. According to Darwin, all living beings had a common ancestor and they diversified over time through small changes.

Darwin's theory was not based on any concrete scientific finding; as he also accepted, it was just an "assumption." Moreover, as Darwin confessed in the long chapter of his book titled "Difficulties of the Theory," the theory was failing in the face of many critical questions.

Darwin invested all his hopes in new scientific discoveries, which he expected to solve the "Difficulties of the Theory." However, contrary to his expectations, scientific findings expanded the dimensions of these difficulties.

The defeat of Darwinism against science can be reviewed under three basic topics:

1) The theory can by no means explain how life originated on the earth.

2) There is no scientific finding showing that the "evolutionary mechanisms" proposed by the theory have any power to evolve at all.

3) The fossil record proves completely the contrary of the suggestions of the theory of evolution.

In this section, we will examine these three basic points in general outlines:

The First Insurmountable Step: The Origin of Life

The theory of evolution posits that all living species evolved from a single living cell that emerged on the primitive earth 3.8 billion years ago. How a single cell could generate millions of complex living species and, if such an evolution really occurred, why traces of it cannot be observed in the fossil record are some of the questions the theory cannot answer. However, first and foremost, of the first step of the alleged evolutionary process it has to be inquired: How did this "first cell" originate?

Since the theory of evolution denies creation and does not accept any kind of supernatural intervention, it maintains that the "first cell" originated coincidentally within the laws of nature, without any design, plan, or arrangement. According to the theory, inanimate matter must have produced a living cell as a result of coincidences. This, however, is a claim inconsistent with even the most unassailable rules of biology.

With the experiments he carried out, Louis Pasteur invalidated the claim that "inanimate matter can create life", which constituted the groundwork of the theory of evolution.

"Life Comes from Life"

In his book, Darwin never referred to the origin of life. The primitive understanding of science in his time rested on the assumption that living beings had a very simple structure. Since medieval times, spontaneous generation, the theory asserting that non-living materials came together to form living organisms, had been widely accepted. It was commonly believed that insects came into being from food leftovers, and mice from wheat. Interesting experiments were conducted to prove this theory. Some wheat was placed on a dirty piece of cloth, and it was believed that mice would originate from it after a while.

Similarly, worms developing in meat was assumed to be evidence of spontaneous generation. However, only some time later was it understood that worms did not appear on meat spontaneously, but were carried there by flies in the form of larvae, invisible to the naked eye.

Even in the period when Darwin wrote *The Origin of Species*, the belief that bacteria could come into existence from non-living matter was widely accepted in the world of science.

However, five years after Darwin's book was published, the discovery of Louis Pasteur disproved this belief, which constituted the groundwork of evolution. Pasteur summarized the conclusion he reached after time-consuming studies and experiments: "The claim that inanimate matter can originate life is buried in history for good."[44]

Advocates of the theory of evolution resisted the findings of Pasteur for a long time. However, as the development of science unraveled the complex structure of the cell of a living being, the idea that life could come into being coincidentally faced an even greater impasse.

Inconclusive Efforts in the 20th Century

The first evolutionist who took up the subject of the origin of life in the 20th century was the renowned Russian biologist Alexander Oparin. With various theses he advanced in the 1930's, he tried to prove that the cell of a living being could originate by coincidence. These studies, however, were doomed to failure, and

Alexander Oparin's attempts to offer an evolutionist explanation for the origin of life ended in a great fiasco.

Oparin had to make the following confession: "Unfortunately, the origin of the cell remains a question which is actually the darkest point of the entire evolution theory."[45]

Evolutionist followers of Oparin tried to carry out experiments to solve the problem of the origin of life. The best known of these experiments was carried out by American chemist Stanley Miller in 1953. Combining the gases he alleged to have existed in the primordial earth's atmosphere in an experiment set-up, and adding energy to the mixture, Miller synthesized several organic molecules (amino acids) present in the structure of proteins.

As accepted also by the latest evolutionist theorists, the origin of life is still a great stumbling block for the theory of evolution.

Barely a few years had passed before it was revealed that this experiment, which was then presented as an important step in the name of evolution, was invalid, the atmosphere used in the experiment having been very different from real earth conditions.[46]

After a long silence, Miller confessed that the atmosphere medium he used was unrealistic.[47]

All the evolutionist efforts put forth throughout the 20th century to explain the origin of life ended with failure. The geochemist Jeffrey Bada from San Diego Scripps Institute accepts this fact in an article published in *Earth* Magazine in 1998:

> Today as we leave the twentieth century, we still face the **biggest unsolved problem that we had when we entered the twentieth century: How did life originate on Earth?**[48]

The Complex Structure of Life

The primary reason why the theory of evolution ended up in such a big impasse about the origin of life is that even the living organisms deemed the simplest have incredibly complex structures. The cell of a living being is more complex than all of the technological products produced by man. Today, even in the most developed laboratories of the world, a living cell cannot be produced by bringing inorganic materials together.

The conditions required for the formation of a cell are too great in quantity to be explained away by coincidences. The probability of proteins, the building blocks of cell, being synthesized coincidentally, is 1 in 10^{950} for an average protein made up of 500 amino acids. In mathematics, a probability smaller than 1 over 10^{50} is practically considered to be impossible.

The DNA molecule, which is located in the nucleus of the cell and which stores genetic information, is an incredible databank. It is calculated that if the information coded in DNA were written down, this would make a giant library consisting of 900 volumes of encyclopaedias of 500 pages each.

A very interesting dilemma emerges at this point: the DNA can only replicate with the help of some specialized proteins (enzymes). However, the synthesis of these enzymes can only be realized by the information coded in DNA. As they both depend on each other, they have to exist at the same time for replication. This brings the scenario that life originated by itself to a deadlock. Prof. Leslie Orgel, an evolutionist of repute from the University of San Diego, California, confesses this fact in the September 1994 issue of the *Scientific American* magazine:

> It is extremely improbable that proteins and nucleic acids, both of which are structurally complex, arose spontaneously in the same place at the same time. Yet it also seems impossible to have one without the other. And so, at first glance, one might have to conclude that life could never, in fact, have originated by chemical means.[49]

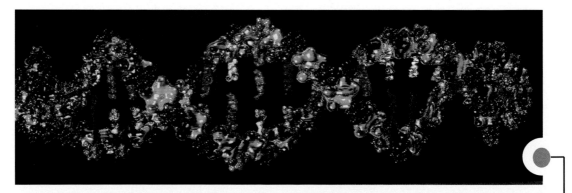

One of the facts nullifying the theory of evolution is the incredibly complex structure of life. The DNA molecule located in the nucleus of cells of living beings is an example of this. The DNA is a sort of databank formed of the arrangement of four different molecules in different sequences. This databank contains the codes of all the physical traits of that living being. When the human DNA is put into writing, it is calculated that this would result in an encyclopaedia made up of 900 volumes. Unquestionably, such extraordinary information definitively refutes the concept of coincidence.

No doubt, if it is impossible for life to have originated from natural causes, then it has to be accepted that life was "created" in a supernatural way. This fact explicitly invalidates the theory of evolution, whose main purpose is to deny creation.

Imaginary Mechanisms of Evolution

The second important point that negates Darwin's theory is that both concepts put forward by the theory as "evolutionary mechanisms" were understood to have, in reality, no evolutionary power.

Darwin based his evolution allegation entirely on the mechanism of "natural selection". The importance he placed on this mechanism was evident in the name of his book: *The Origin of Species, By Means Of Natural Selection...*

Natural selection holds that those living things that are stronger and more suited to the natural conditions of their habitats will survive in the struggle for life. For example, in a deer herd under the threat of attack by wild animals, those that can run faster will survive. Therefore, the deer herd will be comprised of faster and stronger individuals. However, unquestionably, this mechanism will not cause deer to evolve and transform themselves into another living species, for instance, horses.

Therefore, the mechanism of natural selection has no evolutionary power. Darwin was also aware of this fact and had to state this in his book *The Origin of Species*:

Natural selection can do nothing until favourable variations chance to occur.[50]

Lamarck's Impact

So, how could these "favourable variations" occur? Darwin tried to answer this question from the standpoint of the primitive understanding of science in his age. According to the French biologist Lamarck, who lived before Darwin, living creatures passed on the traits they acquired during their lifetime to the next generation and these traits, accumulating from one generation to another, caused new species to be formed. For instance, according to Lamarck, giraffes evolved from antelopes; as they struggled to eat the leaves of high trees, their necks were extended from generation to generation.

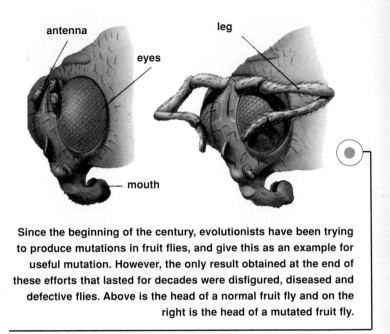

Darwin also gave similar examples, and in his book *The Origin of Species*, for instance, said that some bears going into water to find food transformed themselves into whales over time.[51]

Since the beginning of the century, evolutionists have been trying to produce mutations in fruit flies, and give this as an example for useful mutation. However, the only result obtained at the end of these efforts that lasted for decades were disfigured, diseased and defective flies. Above is the head of a normal fruit fly and on the right is the head of a mutated fruit fly.

However, the laws of inheritance discovered by Mendel and verified by the science of genetics that flourished in the 20th century, utterly demolished the legend that acquired traits were passed on to subsequent generations. Thus, natural selection fell out of favour as an evolutionary mechanism.

Neo-Darwinism and Mutations

In order to find a solution, Darwinists advanced the "Modern Synthetic Theory", or as it is more commonly known, Neo-Darwinism, at the end of the 1930's. Neo-Darwinism added mutations, which are distortions formed in the genes of living beings because of external factors such as radiation or replication errors, as the "cause of favourable variations" in addition to natural mutation.

Today, the model that stands for evolution in the world is Neo-Darwinism. The theory maintains that millions of living beings present on the earth formed as a result of a process whereby numerous complex organs of these organisms such as the ears, eyes, lungs, and wings, underwent "mutations," that is, genetic disorders. Yet, there is an outright scientific fact that totally undermines this theory: **Mutations do not cause living beings to**

The theory of evolution claims that living species gradually evolved from one another. The fossil record, however, explicitly falsifies this claim. For example, in the Cambrian Period, some 550 million years ago, tens of totally distinct living species emerged suddenly. These living beings depicted in the above picture have very complex structures. This fact, referred to as the "Cambrian Explosion" in scientific literature is plain evidence of creation.

develop; on the contrary, they always cause harm to them.

The reason for this is very simple: the DNA has a very complex structure and random effects can only cause harm to it. American geneticist B.G. Ranganathan explains this as follows:

> **Mutations are small, random, and harmful.** They rarely occur and the best possibility is that they will be ineffectual. These four characteristics of mutations imply that mutations cannot lead to an evolutionary development. A random change in a highly specialised organism is either ineffectual or harmful. A random change in a watch cannot improve the watch. It will most probably harm it or at best be ineffectual. An earthquake does not improve the city, it brings destruction.[52]

Not surprisingly, no mutation example, which is useful, that is, which is observed to develop the genetic code, has been observed so far. All mutations have proved to be harmful. It was understood that mutation, which is presented as an "evolutionary mechanism," is actually a genetic occurrence that harms living beings, and leaves them disabled. (The most common effect of mutation on human beings is cancer). No doubt, a destructive mechanism cannot be an "evolutionary mechanism." Natural selection, on the other hand, "can do nothing by itself" as Darwin also accepted. This fact shows us that there is no "evolutionary mechanism" in nature. Since no evolutionary mechanism exists, neither could any imaginary process called evolution have taken place.

The Fossil Record: No Sign of Intermediate Forms

The clearest evidence that the scenario suggested by the theory of evolution did not take place is the fossil record.

According to the theory of evolution, every living species has sprung from a predecessor. A previously existing species turned into something else in time and all species have come into being in this way. According to the theory, this transformation proceeds gradually over millions of years.

Had this been the case, then numerous intermediary species should have existed and lived within this long transformation period.

For instance, some half-fish/half-reptiles should have lived in the past

The fossil record is a great barricade in front of the theory of evolution. The fossil record shows that living species emerged suddenly and fully-formed without any evolutionary transitional form between them. This fact is evidence that species are created separately.

which had acquired some reptilian traits in addition to the fish traits they already had. Or there should have existed some reptile-birds, which acquired some bird traits in addition to the reptilian traits they already had. Since these would be in a transitional phase, they should be disabled, defective, crippled living beings. Evolutionists refer to these imaginary creatures, which they believe to have lived in the past, as **"intermediate forms."**

If such animals had really existed, there should be millions and even billions of them in number and variety. More importantly, the remains of these strange creatures should be present in the fossil record. In *The Origin of Species*, Darwin explained:

> If my theory be true, **numberless intermediate varieties, linking most closely all of the species of the same group together must assuredly have existed...** Consequently, evidence of their former existence could be found only amongst fossil remains.[53]

Darwin's Hopes Shattered

However, although evolutionists have been making strenuous efforts to find fossils since the middle of the 19th century all over the world, no transitional forms have yet been uncovered. All the fossils unearthed in excavations showed that, contrary to the expectations of evolutionists, life appeared on earth all of a sudden and fully-formed.

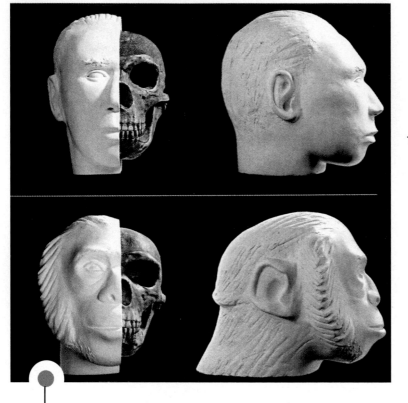

There are no fossil remains that support the tale of human evolution. On the contrary, the fossil record shows that there is an insurmountable barrier between apes and men. In the face of this truth, evolutionists fixed their hopes on certain drawings and models. They randomly place masks on the fossil remains and fabricate imaginary half-ape, half-human faces.

A famous British paleontologist, Derek V. Ager, admits this fact, even though he is an evolutionist:

> The point emerges that if we examine the fossil rec,ord in detail, whether at the level of orders or of species, we find – over and over again – **not gradual evolution, but the sudden explosion of one group at the expense of another.**[54]

This means that in the fossil record, all living species suddenly emerge as fully formed, without any intermediate forms in between. This is just the opposite of Darwin's assumptions. Also, it is very strong evidence that living beings are created. The only explanation of a living species emerging suddenly and complete in every detail without any evolutionary ancestor can be that this species was created. This fact is admitted also by the widely known evolutionist biologist Douglas Futuyma:

> **Creation and evolution, between them, exhaust the possible explanations for the origin of living things.** Organisms either appeared on the earth fully developed or they did not. If they did not, they must have developed from pre-existing species by some process of

modification. If they did appear in a fully developed state, they must indeed have been created by some omnipotent intelligence.[55]

Fossils show that living beings emerged fully developed and in a perfect state on the earth. That means that **"the origin of species" is, contrary to Darwin's supposition, not evolution but creation.**

The Tale of Human Evolution

The subject most often brought up by the advocates of the theory of evolution is the subject of the origin of man. The Darwinist claim holds that the modern men of today evolved from some kind of ape-like creatures. During this alleged evolutionary process, which is supposed to have started 4-5 million years ago, it is claimed that there existed some "transitional forms" between modern man and his ancestors. According to this completely imaginary scenario, four basic "categories" are listed:

1. Australopithecus
2. Homo habilis
3. Homo erectus
4. Homo sapiens

Evolutionists call the so-called first ape-like ancestors of men "Australopithecus" which means "South African ape." These living beings are actually nothing but an old ape species that has become extinct. Extensive research done on various Australopithecus specimens by two world famous anatomists from England and the USA, namely, Lord Solly Zuckerman and Prof. Charles Oxnard, has shown that these belonged to an ordinary ape species that became extinct and bore no resemblance to humans.[56]

Evolutionists classify the next stage of human evolution as "homo," that is "man." According to the evolutionist claim, the living beings in the Homo series are more developed than Australopithecus. Evolutionists devise a fanciful evolution scheme by arranging different fossils of these creatures in a particular order. This scheme is imaginary because it has never been proved that there is an evolutionary relation between these different classes. Ernst Mayr, one of the foremost defenders of the theory of evolution in the 20th century, admits this fact by saying that "the chain reaching as far as Homo sapiens is actually lost."[57]

By outlining the link chain as "Australopithecus > Homo habilis > Homo erectus > Homo sapiens," evolutionists imply that each of these species is one another's ancestor. However, recent findings of paleoanthropologists have revealed that Australopithecus, Homo habilis and Homo erectus lived at different parts of the world at the same time.[58]

Moreover, a certain segment of humans classified as Homo erectus have lived up until very modern times. Homo sapiens neandarthalensis and Homo sapiens sapiens (modern man) co-existed in the same region.[59]

This situation apparently indicates the invalidity of the claim that they are ancestors of one another. A paleontologist from Harvard University, Stephen Jay Gould, explains this deadlock of the theory of evolution although he is an evolutionist himself:

> What has become of our ladder if there are three coexisting lineages of hominids (A. africanus, the robust australopithecines, and H. habilis), none clearly derived from another? Moreover, none of the three display any evolutionary trends during their tenure on earth.[60]

Put briefly, the scenario of human evolution, which is sought to be upheld with the help of various drawings of some "half ape, half human" creatures appearing in the media and course books, that is, frankly, by means of propaganda, is nothing but a tale with no scientific ground.

Lord Solly Zuckerman, one of the most famous and respected scientists in the U.K., who carried out research on this subject for years, and particularly studied Australopithecus fossils for 15 years, finally concluded, despite being an evolutionist himself, that there is, in fact, no such family tree branching out from ape-like creatures to man.

Zuckerman also made an interesting "spectrum of science." He formed a spectrum of sciences ranging from those he considered scientific to those he considered unscientific. According to Zuckerman's spectrum, the most "scientific"–that is, depending on concrete data–fields of science are chemistry and physics. After them come the biological sciences and then the social sciences. At the far end of the spectrum, which is the part considered to be most "unscientific," are "extra-sensory perception"–concepts such as telepathy and sixth sense–and finally "human evolution." Zuckerman explains his reasoning:

We then move right off the register of objective truth into those fields of presumed biological science, like extrasensory perception or the interpretation of man's fossil history, where to the faithful (evolutionist) anything is possible - and where the ardent believer (in evolution) is sometimes able to believe several contradictory things at the same time.[61]

The tale of human evolution boils down to nothing but the prejudiced interpretations of some fossils unearthed by certain people, who blindly adhere to their theory.

Technology In The Eye and The Ear

Another subject that remains unanswered by evolutionary theory is the excellent quality of perception in the eye and the ear.

Before passing on to the subject of the eye, let us briefly answer the question of "how we see". Light rays coming from an object fall oppositely on the retina of the eye. Here, these light rays are transmitted into electric signals by cells and they reach a tiny spot at the back of the brain called the centre of vision. These electric signals are perceived in this centre of the brain as an image after a series of processes. With this technical background, let us do some thinking.

The brain is insulated from light. That means that the inside of the brain is solid dark, and light does not reach the location where the brain is situated. The place called the centre of vision is a solid dark place where no light ever reaches; it may even be the darkest place you have ever known. However, you observe a luminous, bright world in this pitch darkness.

The image formed in the eye is so sharp and distinct that even the technology of the 20th century has not been able to attain it. For instance, look at the book you read, your hands with which you hold it, then lift your head and look around you. Have you ever seen such a sharp and distinct image as this one at any other place? Even the most developed television screen produced by the greatest television producer in the world cannot provide such a sharp image for you. This is a three-dimensional, coloured, and extremely sharp image. For more than 100 years, thousands of engineers have been trying to achieve this sharpness. Factories, huge premises were established, much research has been done, plans and designs have been made for this purpose. Again, look at a TV screen and the book you hold in your hands. You will see that there is a big difference in sharpness and distinction. Moreover, the TV screen shows you a two-dimensional image, whereas with your eyes, you watch a three-dimensional perspective having depth.

For many years, ten of thousands of engineers have tried to make a three-dimensional TV, and reach the vision quality of the eye. Yes, they have made a three-dimensional television system but it is not possible to watch it without putting on glasses; moreover, it is only an artificial three-dimension. The background is more blurred, the foreground appears like a paper setting. Never has it been possible to produce a sharp and distinct vision like that of the eye. In both the camera and the television, there is a loss of image quality.

Evolutionists claim that the mechanism producing this sharp and distinct image has been formed by chance. Now, if somebody told you that the television in your room was formed as a result of chance, that all its atoms just happened to come together and make up this device that produces an image, what would you think? How can atoms do what thousands of people cannot?

If a device producing a more primitive image than the eye could not have been formed by chance, then it is very evident that the eye and the image seen by the eye could not have been formed by chance. The same situation applies to the ear. The outer ear picks up the available sounds by the auricle and directs them to the middle ear; the middle ear transmits the sound vibrations by intensifying them; the inner ear sends these vibrations to the brain by translating them into electric signals. Just as with the eye, the act of hearing finalises in the centre of hearing in the brain.

The situation in the eye is also true for the ear. That is, the brain is insulated from sound just like it is from light: it does not let any sound in. Therefore, no matter how noisy is the outside, the inside of the brain is completely silent. Nevertheless, the sharpest sounds are perceived in the brain. In your brain, which is insulated from sound, you listen to the symphonies of an orchestra, and hear all the noises in a crowded place. However, if the sound level in your brain was measured by a precise device at that moment, it would be seen that a complete silence is prevailing there.

As is the case with imagery, decades of effort have been spent in trying to generate and reproduce sound that is faithful to the original. The results of these efforts are sound recorders, high-fidelity systems, and systems for sensing sound. Despite all this technology and the thousands of engineers and experts who have been working on this endeavour, no sound has yet been obtained that has the same sharpness and clarity as the sound perceived by the ear. Think of the highest-quality HI-FI systems produced by the biggest company in the music industry. Even in these devices, when sound is recorded some of it is lost; or when you turn on a HI-FI you always hear a hissing sound before the music starts. However, the sounds that are the products of the technology of the human body are extremely sharp and clear. A human ear never perceives a sound accompanied by a hissing sound or with atmospherics as does HI-FI; it perceives sound exactly as it is, sharp and clear. This is the way it has been since the creation of man.

So far, no visual or recording apparatus produced by man has been as sensitive and successful in perceiving sensory data as are the eye and the ear.

However, as far as seeing and hearing are concerned, a far greater fact lies beyond all this.

To Whom Does the Consciousness that Sees and Hears Within the Brain Belong?

Who is it that watches an alluring world in its brain, listens to symphonies and the twittering of birds, and smells the rose?

The stimulations coming from the eyes, ears, and nose of a human being travel to the brain as electro-chemical nervous impulses. In biology, physiology, and biochemistry books, you can find many details about how this image forms in the brain. However, you will never come across the most important fact about this subject: Who is it that perceives these electro-chemical nervous impulses as images, sounds, odours and sensory events in the brain? There is a consciousness in the brain that perceives all this without feeling any need for eye, ear, and nose. To whom does this consciousness belong? There is no doubt that this consciousness does not belong to the nerves, the fat layer and neurons comprising the brain. This is why Darwinist-materialists, who believe that everything is comprised of matter, cannot give any answer to these questions.

For this consciousness is the spirit created by God. The spirit needs neither the eye to watch the images, nor the ear to hear the sounds. Furthermore, nor does it need the brain to think.

Everyone who reads this explicit and scientific fact should ponder on Almighty God, should fear Him and seek refuge in Him, He Who squeezes the entire universe in a pitch-dark place of a few cubic centimeters in a three-dimensional, coloured, shadowy, and luminous form.

A Materialist Faith

The information we have presented so far shows us that the theory of evolution is a claim evidently at variance with scientific findings. The theory's claim on the origin of life is inconsistent with science, the evolutionary mechanisms it proposes have no evolutionary power, and fossils demonstrate that the intermediate forms required by the theory never existed. So, it certainly follows that the theory of evolution should be pushed aside as an unscientific idea. This is how many ideas such as the earth-centered universe model have been taken out of the agenda of science throughout history.

However, the theory of evolution is pressingly kept on the agenda of science. Some people even try to represent criticisms directed against the theory as an "attack on science." Why?

The reason is that the theory of evolution is an indispensable dogmatic belief for some circles. These circles are blindly devoted to materialist philosophy and adopt Darwinism because it is the only materialist explanation that can be put forward for the workings of nature.

Interestingly enough, they also confess this fact from time to time. A well known geneticist and an outspoken evolutionist, Richard C. Lewontin from Harvard University, confesses that he is "first and foremost a materialist and then a scientist":

It is not that the methods and institutions of science somehow compel us accept a material explanation of the phenomenal world, but, on the contrary, that **we are forced by our a priori adherence to material causes**

to create an apparatus of investigation and a set of concepts that produce material explanations, no matter how counter-intuitive, no matter how mystifying to the uninitiated. Moreover, that materialism is absolute, so we cannot allow a Divine Foot in the door.[62]

These are explicit statements that Darwinism is a dogma kept alive just for the sake of adherence to the materialist philosophy. This dogma maintains that there is no being save matter. Therefore, it argues that inanimate, unconscious matter created life. It insists that millions of different living species; for instance, birds, fish, giraffes, tigers, insects, trees, flowers, whales and human beings originated as a result of the interactions between matter such as the pouring rain, the lightning flash, etc., out of inanimate matter. This is a precept contrary both to reason and science. Yet Darwinists continue to defend it just so as "not to allow a Divine Foot in the door."

Anyone who does not look at the origin of living beings with a materialist prejudice will see this evident truth: All living beings are works of a Creator, Who is All-Powerful, All-Wise and All-Knowing. This Creator is God, Who created the whole universe from non-existence, designed it in the most perfect form, and fashioned all living beings.

They said 'Glory be to You!
We have no knowledge except what You have taught us.
You are the All-Knowing, the All-Wise.'
(Qur'an, 2:32)

NOTES

Foreword by Aftab Ahmad Malik

1. Lawrence H Sear, Managing editor of The Daily Mail writing in a column in *The News International*, November 21, 2001, page 10

2. "Islam Attracts Converts by the Thousands, Drawn Before and After Attacks" October 22, 2001, *New York Times*; Jodi Wilgoren

3. J. L. Esposito, *The Islamic Threat – Myth or Reality?* New York and Oxford: Oxford University Press, 1992, p.173

4. "The True Peaceful Face of Islam" *TIME* Magazine, October 1, 2001 Vol. 158 No. 15; Karen Armstrong

5. Nasr, Seyyed Hossein, *Islam and the plight of Modern Man*, Suhail Academy, Lahore, 1999, p 122

6. Although the world of Islam is viewed as being distinct and separate from the European world – the former world was inextricably linked with the development of the West. Muslim scholars have made vital contributions in the sphere of the sciences, arts and scholasticism which have formed the foundation of modern civilisation. Despite such contributions, most of the Western world are unaware of such luminaries as: Ibn Sina (Avicenna) b 980AD, who wrote al-Qanun (The Canon) which was one of the most influential medical textbooks in medieval Europe until the 17th century. Ibn al-Nafis (d. 1289) who explained blood flow, over three hundred years before William Harvey, who wrote about it in 1628. Jabir Ibn Haiyan (Geber), known as the father of chemistry. The very name Chemistry is derived from the Arabic al-Kimya. Several technical terms introduced by Jabir, such as Alkali, Cinnabar and alembic are still used in modern scientific vocabulary. Muhammad Bin Musa al- Khawarizimi (Algorizam) introduced the mathematical concept of algorithm, which is named after his last name. He is the recognised founder of algebra, which is the name derived from his famous book – *al-Jabbr Wa-al Muqabilah*. This book was the principal mathematical textbook in European universities until the 16th century. See: Beckingham, C.F., Misconceptions of Islam: Medieval and Modern, *Journal of Royal Society of Arts*, September 1976; Draper, John William, *The Intellectual Development of Europe* (London) Vol. I, 1875; Makdisi, George, *The Rise Of Humanism In Classical Islam & The Christian West* (Edinburgh) 1991; W. Montgomery Watt, *Islamic Surveys*; *The Influence of Islam on Medieval Europe* (Edinburgh) 1972

7. http://66.34.131.5/ISLAM/ahm/recapturing.htm

8. Asqalani, Ibn Hajar, Fath al-Bari, 1.194 hadith 100

9. "Terrorism Is at Odds With Islamic Tradition" *The Los Angeles Times*; August 22, 2001; Khaled Abou El-Fadl

10. Al-Buti, Muhammad Sa'id, Jihad in Islam: *How to understand and practise it*, (Ed.Absi, Munzer Adel) Dar al Fikr (Damascus) 1995

11. "Jihad: It's no free ticket to Violence" The London Free Press, Nov. 5/01; Munir Abu Muhammad El-Kassem,

12. As related by Tabrizi, Mishkat, Vol. II, hadith 4998

13. "On The Concept of Compassion In Islam" Institute of Islamic Studies, Mumbai (Bombay) Islam and Modern Age, November, 2001, Asghar Ali Engineer

14. What drives people to hate the U.S. enough to wreak death, destruction and carnage upon its innocent population? Although writing three years ago, Graham E. Fuller made a point that still holds true today. He wrote: ' [I]t is dangerous to divorce terrorism from politics, yet the U.S. media continue to talk about an abstract war against terrorism without mention of the issues or context that lie behind them'. Graham E. Fuller, 'Air-strikes Aren't the Endgame', *Los Angeles Times*, August 24, 1998

15. "Muslims Abhor The Double Standard" *Los Angeles Times*, 5 October 2001; Graham E. Fuller

16. http://66.34.131.5/ISLAM/ahm/recapturing.htm

Islam Denounces Terrorism

1. Prof. Thomas Arnold, *The Spread of Islam in the World, A History of Peaceful Preaching*, Goodword Books, 2001, p. 79-80

2. John L. Esposito, *Islam: The Straight Path*, Oxford University Press, 1998, p. 10

3. Ahmad Diya'al-Din al-Kamushkhanawi, *Ramuz al-Ahadith*, Vol 1, 84/8

4. Ahmad Diya'al-Din al-Kamushkhanawi, *Ramuz al-Ahadith*, Vol 1, 76/12

5. *Bukhari* (5778) and *Muslim* (109 and 110), Reported by Muslim - Eng. Trans, Vol. 1, p.62, No. 203

6. Karen Armstrong, *Holy War*, MacMillan London Limited, 1988, p. 25

7. Tabari, *Ta' rikh*, 1, 1850, cited in Majid Khadduri, *War and Peace in the Law of Islam*, Johns Hopkins Press, Baltimore, 1955, p. 102

8. W.H.C. Frend, "Christianity in the Middle East: Survey Down to A.D. 1800", Religion in the Middle East, Ed. A.J. Arberry, I-II Cambridge, 1969, Volume I, p. 289

9. Prof. Thomas Arnold, *The Spread of Islam in the World, A History of Peaceful Preaching*, p. 71-72

10. L. Browne, *The Prospects of Islam*, p. 11-15

11. John L. Esposito, *Islam: The Straight Path*, p. 33-34

12. Bernard Lewis, *The Middle East*, Weidenfeld & Nicolson, London, 1995, p. 210

13. Prof. Thomas Arnold, *The Spread of Islam in the World, A History of Peaceful Preaching*, p. 96

14. Prof. Thomas Arnold, *The Spread of Islam in the World, A History of Peaceful Preaching*, p. 88-89

15. Ekmeleddin Ihsanoglu (ed.), Osmanlı Devleti ve Medeniyeti Tarihi (The History of the Ottoman State and Civilization), IRCICA, Istanbul, 1994, p. 467

16. *Gesta Francorum, or the Deeds of the Franks and the Other Pilgrims to Jerusalem*, translated by Rosalind Hill, London, 1962, p. 91

17. August C. Krey, *The First Crusade: The Accounts of Eye-Witnesses and Participants*, Princeton & London, 1921, p. 261

18. August C. Krey, *The First Crusade: The Accounts of Eye-Witnesses and Participants*, p. 262

19. Alan Ereira, David Wallace, *Crusades: Terry Jones Tells the Dramatic Story of Battle for Holy Land*, BBC World Wide Ltd., 1995.

20. The Pact of Najran, Article 6, http://www.islamic resources.com/Pact_of_Najran.htm

21. Karen Armstrong, *Holy War*, p. 30-31

22. John L. Esposito, *Islam: The Straight Path*, p. 58

23. Prof. Thomas Arnold, *The Spread of Islam in the World, A History of Peaceful Preaching*, p. 56

24. John L. Esposito, *Islam: The Straight Path*, p. 59

25. Karen Armstrong, *Holy War*, p. 185

26. Francis E. Peters, Jerusalem: Holy City in the Eyes of Chroniclers, Visitors, Pilgrims, and Prophets from the Days of Abraham to the Beginnings of Modern Times, Princeton, Princeton University Press, 1985, p. 363

27. An Interview with Edward Said by the Israeli Newspaper *Haaretz*, Friday, August 18, 2000

28. Charles Darwin, *The Descent of Man*, 2nd edition, New York, A L. Burt Co., 1874, p. 178

29. Lalita Prasad Vidyarthi, *Racism, Science and Pseudo-Science*, Unesco, France, Vendôme, 1983. p. 54

30. Theodore D. Hall, "The Scientific Backgro-und of the Nazi "Race Purification" Program", http://www.trufax.org/avoid/nazi.html

31. James Joll, *Europe Since 1870: An International History*, Penguin Books, Middlesex, 1990, p. 164

32. M.F. Ashley-Montagu, Man in Process, New York: World. Pub. Co. 1961, pp. 76, 77 cited in Bolton Davidheiser, W E Lammers (ed) Scientific Studies in Special Creationism, 1971, p. 338-339

33. L.H. Gann, "Adolf Hitler, The Complete Totalitarian", *The Intercollegiate Review*, Fall 1985, p. 24; cited in Henry M. Morris, *The Long war Against God*, Baker Book House, 1989, p. 78

34. J. Tenenbaum., *Race and Reich*, Twayne Pub., New York, p. 211, 1956; cited by Jerry Bergman, "Darwinism and the Nazi Race Holocaust", http://www.trueorigin. org/holocaust.htm

Totalitarian", *The Intercollegiate Review*, Fall 1985, p. 24; cited in Henry M. Morris, *The Long war Against God*, Baker Book House, 1989, p. 78

34. J. Tenenbaum., *Race and Reich*, Twayne Pub., New York, p. 211, 1956; cited by Jerry Bergman, "Darwinism and the Nazi Race Holocaust", http://www.trueorigin. org/holocaust.htm

35. Peter Chrisp, *The Rise Of Fascism*, Witness History Series, p. 6

36. Hickman, R., *Biocreation*, Science Press, Worthington, OH, pp. 51–52, 1983; Jerry Bergman, "Darwinism and the Nazi Race Holocaust", Creation Ex Nihilo Technical Journal 13 (2): 101–111, 1999

37. Robert M. Young, *Darwinian Evolution and Human History*, Historical Studies on Science and Belief, 1980

38. Alan Woods and Ted Grant, *Reason in Revolt: Marxism and Modern Science*, London: 1993

39. K. Mehnert, *Kampf um Mao's Erbe*, Deutsche Verlags-Anstalt, 1977

40. Karl Marx, *Das Capital*, Vol. I, 1955, p. 603

41. Vladimir Ilich Lenin, *Collected Works*, 4th English Edition, Progress Publishers, Moscow, 1965, Volume 11, p. 216

42. L. Poliakov, *Le Mythe Aryen*, Editions Complexe, Calmann-Lévy, Bruxelles, 1987, p. 343

43. Robert Clark, *Darwin: Before and After*, Grand Rapids International Press, Grand Rapids, MI, 1958., s. 115-116; cited by Jerry Bergman, "Darwinism and the Nazi Race Holocaust", http://www.trueorigin.org/holocaust.htm

44. Sidney Fox, Klaus Dose, *Molecular Evolution and The Origin of Life*, New York: Marcel Dekker, 1977. p. 2

45. Alexander I. Oparin, *Origin of Life*, (1936) New York, Dover Publications, 1953 (Reprint), p.196

46. "New Evidence on Evolution of Early Atmosphere and Life", *Bulletin of the American Meteorological Society*, vol 63, November 1982, p. 1328-1330.

47. Stanley Miller, Molecular Evolution of Life: Current Status of the Prebiotic Synthesis of Small Molecules, 1986, p. 7

48. Jeffrey Bada, *Earth*, February 1998, v. 40

49. Leslie E. Orgel, "The Origin of Life on Earth", *Scientific American*, vol 271, October 1994, p. 78

50. Charles Darwin, *The Origin of Species: A Facsimile of the First Edition*, Harvard University Press, 1964, p. 189

51. Charles Darwin, *The Origin of Species*, p. 184.

52. B. G. Ranganathan, *Origins?*, Pennsylvania: The Banner Of Truth Trust, 1988.

53. Charles Darwin, *The Origin of Species*, p. 179

54. Derek A. Ager, "The Nature of the Fossil Record", Proceedings of the British Geological Association, vol 87, 1976, p. 133

55. Douglas J. Futuyma, *Science on Trial*, New York: Pantheon Books, 1983. p. 197

56. Solly Zuckerman, *Beyond The Ivory Tower*, New York: Toplinger Publications, 1970, ss. 75-94; Charles E. Oxnard, "The Place of Australopithecines in Human Evolution: Grounds for Doubt", Nature, vol 258, p. 389

57. J. Rennie, "Darwin's Current Bulldog: Ernst Mayr", *Scientific American*, December 1992

58. Alan Walker, *Science*, vol. 207, 1980, p. 1103; A. J. Kelso, Physical Antropology, 1st ed., New York: J. B. Lipincott Co., 1970, s. 221; M. D. Leakey, Olduvai Gorge, vol. 3, Cambridge: Cambridge University Press, 1971, p. 272

59. *Time*, November 1996

60. S. J. Gould, *Natural History*, vol. 85, 1976, p. 30

61. Solly Zuckerman, *Beyond The Ivory Tower*, p. 19

62. Richard Lewontin, "Billions and billions of demons", *The New York Review of Books*, 9 January, 1997, p. 28.

Also by Harun Yahya

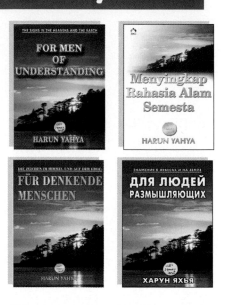

Many people think that Darwin's Theory of Evolution is a proven fact. Contrary to this conventional wisdom, recent developments in science completely disprove the theory. The only reason Darwinism is still foisted on people by means of a worldwide propaganda campaign lies in the ideological aspects of the theory. All secular ideologies and philosophies try to provide a basis for themselves by relying on the theory of evolution.

This book clarifies the scientific collapse of the theory of evolution in a way that is detailed but easy to understand. It reveals the frauds and distortions committed by evolutionists to "prove" evolution. Finally it analyzes the powers and motives that strive to keep this theory alive and make people believe in it.

Anyone who wants to learn about the origin of living things, including mankind, needs to read this book. *The Evolution Deceit* is also available in Italian, Albanian, Spanish, Indonesian, Malay Russian and Serbo-Croat (Bosnian).

When a person examines his own body or any other living thing in nature, the world or the whole universe, in it he sees a great design, art, plan and intelligence. All this is evidence proving God's being, unit, and eternal power.

For Men of Understanding was written to make the reader see and realise some of the evidence of creation in nature. *For Men of Understanding* is also available in Indonesian, German and Russian.

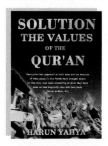

People who are oppressed, who are tortured to death, innocent babies, those who cannot afford even a loaf of bread, who must sleep in tents or even in streets in cold weather, those who are massacred just because they belong to a certain tribe, women, children, and old people who are expelled from their homes because of their religion… Eventually, there is only one solution to the injustice, chaos, terror, massacres, hunger, poverty, and oppression: the morals of the Qur'an.

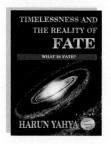

How was matter and time created from nothingness? What does the Big Bang theory signify about the creation of the universe? What is the parallelism between Einstein's Theory of Relativity and the Qur'anic verses?

All of these questions are answered in this book. If you want to learn the truths about space, matter, time and fate, read this book.

We fall sick many times throughout our lives. When the events of "sickness" and "recovering" take place, our bodies become a battleground in which a bitter struggle is taking place. Microbes invisible to our eyes intrude into our body and begin to increase rapidly. The body however has a mechanism that combats them. Known as the "immune system", this mechanism is the most disciplined, most complex and successful army of the world. This system proves that the human body is the outcome of a unique design that has been planned with a great wisdom and skill. In other words, the human body is the evidence of a flawless creation, which is the peerless creation of God.

In a body that is made up of atoms, you breathe in air, eat food, and drink liquids that are all composed of atoms. Everything you see is nothing but the result of the collision of electrons of atoms with photons.
In this book, the implausibility of the spontaneous formation of an atom, the building-block of everything, living or non-living, is related and the flawless nature of God's creation is demonstrated.

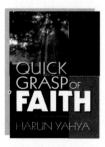

There are questions about religion that people seek answers to and hope to be enlightened in the best way. However in most cases, people base their opinions on hearsay rather than acquiring them from the real source of religion: the Qur'an. In these booklets, you will find the most accurate answers to all the questions you seek answers for and learn your responsibilities towards your Creator.

This book deals with how the theory of evolution is invalidated by scientific findings and experiments in a concise and simple language.

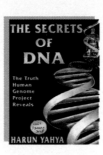

Scientific progress makes it clear that living beings have an extremely complex structure and an order that is too perfect to have come into being by accident. Recently, for example, the perfect structure in the human gene became a top issue as a result of hte completion of the Human Genome Project. In this book, the unique creation of God is once again disclosed for all to see.

Just as a tiny key opens a huge door, this book will open new horizons for its readers. And the reality behind that door is the most important reality that one can come across in one's lifetime. Relating the amazing and admirable features of spiders known by few people and asking the questions of "how" and "why" in the process, this book reveals the excellence and perfection inherent in God's creation.

In the Qur'an, conscience has a meaning and importance beyond its common and everyday use. This book introduces the real concept of conscience that is related in the Qur'an and draws our attention to the kind of understanding, thought, and wisdom that a truly conscientious person has.

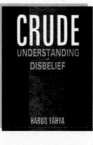

God, in the Qur'an, calls the culture of people who are not subject to the religion of God "ignorance." Only a comparison of this culture with the honourable thoughts and moral structure of the Qur'an can reveal its primitive and corrupted nature. The purpose of this book is to take this comparison further, displaying the extent of the "crude understanding" of ignorant societies.

"Everything that constitutes our life is a totality of perceptions received by our soul. The things, people, places and events that make our world and our lives meaningful are like a dream; we perceive them only as images in our brain, and have nothing to do with their truth or reality…"

In the book, which consists of a conversation between four people, the prejudices that prevent people from understanding this great truth are removed, and the misconceptions they have are explained.

The plan, design, and delicate balance existing in our bodies and reaching into even the remotest corners of the incredibly vast universe must surely have a superior Creator. Man is unable to see his Creator yet he can nevertheless grasp His existence, strength, and wisdom by means of his intellect. This book is a summons to think. A summons to ponder over the universe and living beings and see how they have been created flawlessly.

In the Qur'an, God tells people many secrets. People who are unaware of these secrets experience the trouble and distress caused by this throughout their lives. For those who learn these secrets of the Qur'an, however, the life of this world is very easy, and full of joy and excitement. This book deals with the subjects God related to people as a secret.

One of the principal deceptions that impels people into delinquency and makes them pursue their own desires is their heedlessness of death. Both human beings and the universe they live in are mortal. What awaits the disbelievers in the next world is more dreadful: the eternal wrath of hell. This book, based on the verses of the Qur'an, makes a detailed depiction of the moment of death, the day of judgement, and the penalties in hell, and it sounds a warning about the great danger facing us. Death Resurrection Hell is also available in Polish.

The Qur'an has been sent down as a book easily understandable to everyone. Everyone who believes in God and follows his conscience can take counsel from the verses of the Qur'an and obey the commands in the verses. However, those who follow their lower self fail to measure God with His true scale, entertain doubts about the hereafter, interpret the verses of the Qur'an wrongly in their own crooked reasoning. In this book, the reasons why those who do not use their intellect misinterpret the Qur'an are examined and some examples of the unwise interpretations and objections they make concerning the verses are reviewed and answered.

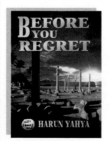

The purpose of this book is to warn people against the day on which they will say "If only we did not rebel against God. If only we listened to the messengers…" and therefore feel deep regret. This is a summons to live for the cause of God when there is still time.

The way to examine the universe and all the beings therein and to discover God's art of creation and announce it to humanity is "science". Therefore, religion adopts science as a way to reach the details of God's creation and therefore encourages science. Just as religion encourages scientific research, so does scientific research that is guided by the facts communicated by religion yield very repid and definite results. This is because religion is the unique source that provides the most correct and definite answer to the question of how the universe and life came into being.

Fascism and communism, which made humanity suffer dark times, are considered to be opposed ideas. However, these ideologies are fed from the same source, on the grounds of which they can attract masses to their side. This source has never drawn attention, always remaining behind the scenes. This source is the materialist philosophy and its adaptation to nature, which is DARWINISM. The acknowledgement of the scientific invalidity of this theory that serves as a basis for cruel dictators and vicious ideological trends will bring about the end of all these detrimental ideologies.

Colours, patterns, spots even lines of each living being existing in nature have a meaning. An attentive eye would immediately recognise that not only the living beings, but also everything in nature are just as they should be. Furthermore, he would realise that everything is given to the service of man: the comforting blue colour of the sky, the colourful view of flowers, the bright green trees and meadows, the moon and stars illuminating the world in pitch darkness together with innumerable beauties surrounding man *Allah's Artistry in Colour* is also available in Arabic.

The unprecedented style and the superior wisdom inherent in the Qur'an is conclusive evidence confirming that it is the Word of God. Apart from this, there are a number of miracles verifying the fact that the Qur'an is the revelation of God, one of them being that, 1,400 years ago, it declared a number of scientific facts that have only been established thanks to the technological breakthroughs of the 20th century. In this book, in addition to the scientific miracles of the Qur'an, you will also find messages regarding the future. Mracles of the Qur'an is also available in Serbo-Croat (Bosnian).

Darwin said: "If it could be demonstrated that any complex organ existed, which could not possibly have been formed by numerous, successive, slight modifications, my theory would absolutely break down." When you read this book, you will see that Darwin's theory has absolutely broken down, just as he feared it would.

A thorough examination of the feathers of a bird, the sonar system of a bat or the wing structure of a fly reveal amazingly complex designs. And these designs indicate that they are created flawlessly by God.

Never plead ignorance of God's evident existence, that everything was created by God, that everything you own was given to you by God for your subsistence, that you will not stay so long in this world, of the reality of death, that the Qur'an is the Book of truth, that you will give account for your deeds, of the voice of your conscience that always invites you to righteousness, of the existence of the hereafter and the day of account, that hell is the eternal home of severe punishment, and of the reality of fate.

The world is a temporary place specially created by God to test man. That is why, it is inherently flawed and far from satisfying man's endless needs and desires. Each and every attraction existing in the world eventually wears out, becomes corrupt, decays and finally disappears. This is the never-changing reality of life.

This book explains this most important essence of life and leads man to ponder the real place to which he belongs, namely the Hereafter.

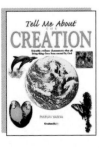

Darwin's theory of evolution maintained that all living beings emerged as a result of chance coincidence and thus denied Creation. Yet, scientific developments did not favour the evolutionist standpoint and simply opposed it. Different branches of science like biochemistry, genetics, and palaeontology have demonstrated that the claims that life originated as a result of "coincidences" is foolish. This is a book you will read with pleasure and as it makes explicitly clear why the theory of evolution is the greatest aberration in the history of science.

Man is a being to which God has granted the faculty of thinking. Yet a majority of people fail to employ this faculty as they should… The purpose of this book is to summon people to think in the way they should and to guide them in their efforts to think. This book is also available in Indonesian.

These millimeter-sized animals that we frequently come across but don't care much about have an excellent ability for organization and specialization that is not to be matched by any other being on earth. These aspects of ants create in one a great admiration for God's superior power and unmatched creation.

Many societies that rebelled against the will of God or regarded His messengers as enemies were wiped off the face of the earth completely... *Perished Nations* examines these penalties as revealed in the verses of the Quran and in light of archaeological discoveries. This book is also available in German, French, Spanish, Russian and Portuguese.

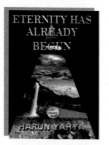

In this book you will find explanations about eternity, timelessness and spacelessness that you will never have encountered anywhere else and you will be confronted by the reality that eternity has already begun. The real answers to many questions people always ponder such as the true nature of death, resurrection after death, the existence of an eternal life, and the time when all these things will happen are to be found here…

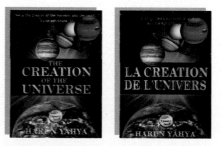

Today, science has proven that the universe was created from nothing with a Big Bang. Moreover, all physical balances of the universe are designed to support human life. Everything from the nuclear reactions in stars to the chemical properties of a carbon atom or a water molecule, is created in a glorious harmony. This is the exalted and flawless creation of God, the Lord of All the Worlds. *The Creation of the Universe* is also available in French.

While watching television or reading the paper, you see many items which you do would not like to see or hear: destitute people, murders, quarrels, ill-treatment, and much more... Certainly, you, too, would like to live in a peaceful and secure society where people live in harmony and friendship. However just waiting for such a world to come about by itself one day is of no use. This book is a summons to those who want goodness to prevail: it calls on them to do goodness and to form an alliance with other good people like themselves.

HARUN YAHYA ON THE INTERNET

YOU CAN FIND ALL THE WORKS OF HARUN YAHYA ON THE INTERNET

• Scientific refutation of Darwinism, the greatest deception of our age.

• Dozens of books including hundreds of pages of information about the signs of God's creation.

• Extremely valuable works that will guide you to think on the real aspects of life by reading the morals of the Qur'an.

• Harun Yahya's political, scientific and faith-related articles that have appeared in various magazines and newspapers around the world.

• Audio recordings and documentary videos inspired by the works of Harun Yahya.

• And many more attractive presentations...

www.harunyahya.com - www.hyahya.org
e-mail: info@harunyahya.com

Islam is a religion that means "peace". In the Qur'an, the Holy Book of Islam, God commands believers to bring peace and security to the world. Terrorism and all other mischief on Earth are the very acts that Muslims are commanded by God to stand against. The Islamic morality is the cure for terrorism, not the source of it. This website is launched to reveal that any kind of terror and barbarism is against Islam, and Muslims share the sorrows of the victims of terrorism.

www.islamdenouncesterrorism.com
e-mail: info@islamdenouncesterrorism.com

Anti-semitism is a fanatical hatred felt for the Jewish people. This racist ideology has caused millions of Jews to be killed, persecuted, exiled and threatened. The religion of Islam aims to bring justice to the world. Just as it denounces all kinds of racism, so it denounces anti-semitism. Muslims criticize Zionism, but defend the right of Jews to live in peace and security.

www.islamdenouncesantisemitism.com
e-mail: info@islamdenouncesantisemitism.com

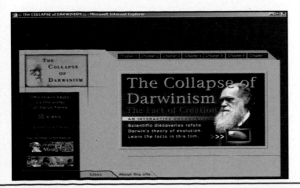

This site is part of a chain of sites set up parallel to Harun Yahya's official homepage (www.harunyahya.com). This site is intended to inform the whole world of some important truths. The most important of these truths is the fact of creation: Life and man did not emerge by themselves, as a result of chance, as materialist philosophy claims. In the same way that God created the universe from nothing, He also created and gave shape to living things and man. This is a fact backed up by contemporary scientific discoveries. In this site is a documentary that genuinely explains the truth of creation.

www.evolutiondocumentary.com
e-mail: info@evolutiondocumentary.com

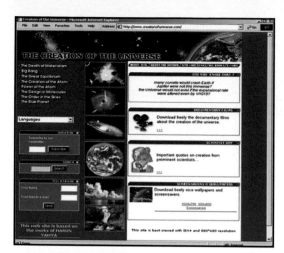

You will read all the details about the creation of the universe in this site

Today, science shows that the universe was created with a Big Bang from nothing in a single moment. You will read everything you would like to know about the perfect creation of the universe in this site. Besides, you can also find in this site the stages that took place from the Big Bang until our day, illustrated by striking photographs.

www.creationofuniverse.com
e-mail: info@creationofuniverse.com

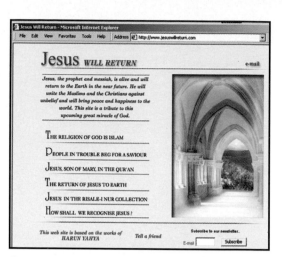

Read about this divine blessing which only a minority of people will enjoy

In the history of mankind, the fact that Jesus (as) will be sent back to Earth for a second time by God is surely a divine blessing to all humanity. Only a minority of people will enjoy this occasion. In this site, you will find all the interesting facts about Jesus' return to Earth.

www.jesuswillreturn.com
e-mail: info@jesuswillreturn.com

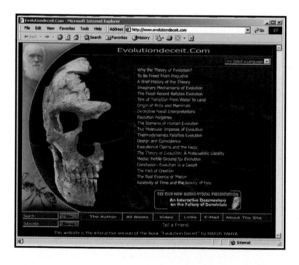

The well-known work of Harun Yahya is now on the Internet!

Harun Yahya's The Evolution Deceit, which has been translated into 6 languages so far, is now available on the Internet with additional updates. You will find all the deadlocks of the theory of evolution on this site.

www.evolutiondeceit.com
e-mail: info@evolutiondeceit.com

Striking examples from the lives of the past nations

This site explores some nations which were destroyed due to their rebellion against God and their denial of His Prophets. The purpose of the site is to reveal the manifestations of the Qur'anic verses which give an account of these events and prove once more that the Qur'an is the word of God. Besides, it is also intended that all these incidents, each of which is an "example to their own time", can serve as a "warning".

www.perishednations.com
e-mail: info@perishednations.com

In the Qur'an, there is an explicit reference to the "second coming of the Jesus to the world" which is heralded in a hadith. The realisation of some information revealed in the Qur'an about Jesus can only be possible by Jesus' second coming…

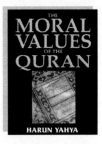

A study that examines and seeks to remind us of the basic moral principles of the Qur'an, particularly those that are most likely to be forgotten or neglected at times.

The Qur'an has been revealed to us so that we may read and ponder. The Basic Concepts of the Qur'an is a useful resource prepared as a guide to thinking. Some basic Islamic concepts like the soul, conscience, wisdom, loyalty, submission to God, brotherhood, modesty, prayer, patience, are discussed in the light of Qur'anic verses. This book is also available in Portuguese.

The most serious mistake a man makes is not pondering. It is not possible to find the truth unless one thinks about basic questions such as "How and why am I here?", "Who created me?", or "Where am I going?." Failing to do so, one becomes trapped in the vicious circle of daily life and turns into a selfish creature caring only for himself. *Ever Thought About the Truth?* summons people to think on such basic questions and to discover the real meaning of life. This book is also available in French.

In order for justice to reign on the Earth, a morality that will make people leave their own interests aside in favour of justice is needed. This morality is the Qur'anic morality that God teaches and commands us. In Surat an-Nisa, God commands believers to act justly, albeit against themselves. The purpose of this book is to describe the true justice in the Qur'an.

These books, prepared for kids, are about the miraculous characteristics of the living things on the Earth. Full colour and written in a concise style, these books give your children the opportunity to get to know God and His perfect artistry in creation. *The World of Our Little Friends: The Ants* is also available in Russian.

Children!
Have you ever asked yourself questions like these: How did our earth come into existence? How did the moon and sun come into being? Where were you before you were born? How did oceans, trees, animals appear on earth? How does a little tiny bee know how to produce delicious honey? How can it build a honeycomb with such astonishingly regular edges? Who was the first human being? In this book you will find the true answers to these questions.

VIDEO FILMS

The works of Harun Yahya are also produced in the form of documentary films and audio cassettes. In addition to English, some of these products are also available in English, Arabic, German, and Russian.

THE FACT OF CREATION
AUDIO CASSETTE SERIES

The titles in this series include The Theory of Evolution The Fact of Creation, The Creation of the Universe/The Balances in the Earth, The Miracle in the Cell/The Miracle of Birth, The Miracle in the Eye/The Miracle in the Ear, The Design in Animals/The Design in Plants, The Miracle in the Honeybee/The Miracle in the Ant, The Miracle in the Mosquito/The Miracle in the Spider, Self-Sacrifice in Living Things/Migration and Orientation, The Miracle of Creation in DNA, Miracles of the Qur'an.

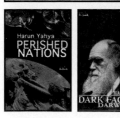

The audio cassettes Perished Nations and The Dark Face of Darwin were inspired by the works of Harun Yahya

The Collapse of Evolution The Fact of Creation audio cassette is also available in Russian.